Table Of Contents

Conclusion

Introduction: The Tribes Among Us

Tribalism, though often masked as a natural human instinct for belonging, carries a shadow that has haunted societies for centuries. Beyond its veneer of camaraderie and shared identity lies a force capable of tearing civilizations apart. Wars that have scarred history's pages rarely began without the seed of tribalism taking root. From the territorial disputes of ancient empires to the ideological clashes of modern geopolitics, the essence of "us versus them" has fueled countless conflicts. It is tribalism that paints neighbors as enemies and strangers as threats, replacing understanding with suspicion and dialogue with discord.

But the scars of tribalism are not confined to battlefields. In the everyday rhythm of life, it sows seeds of communication breakdowns and misunderstandings. Words are misinterpreted, motives questioned, and assumptions hardened—all because people view others through the narrow lens of their tribe. Families are divided, friendships severed, and communities fractured, not by insurmountable differences, but by the unwillingness to cross tribal lines. In boardrooms and classrooms, churches and homes, tribalism whispers the lie that loyalty to a group is more important than the truth or the greater good.

This pervasive force infects more than just human interactions. Tribalism stifles progress, halting the flow of innovation and collaboration. It builds silos in workplaces, where departments cling to their methods rather than seek solutions together. It infiltrates politics, turning debates into shouting matches and reducing complex issues into stark dichotomies. Tribalism fosters a slew of societal ills: prejudice, exclusion, and even hatred. In its grip, the ability to see beyond differences fades, replaced by a reflex to defend one's own tribe at all costs.

The consequences are undeniable, yet the pull of tribalism remains. It promises security and identity, wrapping itself in the comforting cloak of shared values and common enemies. But this promise is deceptive, for tribalism divides far more than it unites. Beneath its allure lies a reality that weakens the very foundations of society, eroding trust, mutual respect, and the pursuit of peace.

It is within this tension that the story of tribalism unfolds—a force that both connects and divides, comforts and destroys. As the world grows smaller through technology and globalization, tribalism has not diminished but evolved, finding new ways to entrench itself in the fabric of life.

In the quiet hum of daily life, tribalism whispers its subtle call. It lurks in the charged energy of a political rally, where chants echo through the air like battle cries, and banners become shields of allegiance. It sits heavy at family gatherings, the unspoken tension of differing views weaving an invisible barrier between loved ones. Even in the most mundane exchanges—online debates, workplace chatter, or casual social interactions—tribalism pulses beneath the surface, shaping words, thoughts, and choices. The pull to align with a group, to find belonging within the safety of shared identity, is both instinctive and powerful.

Yet, this longing for connection often comes at a cost. The lines drawn between "us" and "them" are rarely benign. They slice through friendships, sever bonds, and create chasms in places once defined by unity. Like invisible walls, these divisions rise in homes, churches, and communities, leaving behind fragments of what once was whole. Tribalism feeds on the human desire for certainty, offering a seductive simplicity: you belong here, and they do not. But in doing so, it blinds us to the beauty of even nuanced diversity, the richness of dialogue, and the call to love beyond boundaries.

The modern world has become a fertile ground for tribalism to thrive. Social media platforms, with their endless feeds of curated opinions, fuel the fire, reinforcing echo chambers that deepen divides. Political rhetoric stirs emotions into storms, painting opposing views as threats rather than differences to be understood. Even the Church, called to reflect the unity of Christ, finds itself fractured by denominational allegiances and doctrinal disputes. Tribalism, though ancient in its origins, wears a modern guise, infiltrating every aspect of life.

This book begins with the reality of these lines. It seeks to unravel the threads of tribalism that bind and divide, to understand its origins and implications. More importantly, it aims to explore how tribalism shapes our relationships, communities, and faith. What is it about this need to belong that compels us to cling so tightly to our tribes, and at what cost? Is there a way to transcend the walls we've built, to find unity in the midst of diversity?

This book is written through the lens of a moral and scientifically grounded perspective; it is rooted in reflections that draw from a variety of sources. However, its key points and insights are universally accessible, transcending any specific worldview or belief system. The central truths about human nature, the impact of tribalism, and the call for unity resonate across all perspectives, offering wisdom and clarity to readers regardless of their background. The purpose of this book is to foster understanding and inspire meaningful dialogue that bridges divides, no matter where one stands.

As the pages turn, you will be invited to journey through history and the complexities of modern life. Together, we will confront the shadows tribalism casts over society and uncover the light of hope that still shines. For in recognizing the divisions among us, there is an opportunity—a chance to reclaim unity, to build bridges where there are walls, and to seek belonging not in exclusion, but in love. This is where the journey begins....

Ancient Roots of Tribalism

The story of tribalism begins in the shadow of an ancient tower. According to the biblical narrative of the Tower of Babel, humanity once spoke a single language, unified in purpose and ambition. Together, they sought to build a tower that reached the heavens—a monument to their collective identity and shared power. But this unity was born of pride, a desire not to glorify something greater but to make a name for themselves. In response, the story tells of how their language was confounded, scattering them across the earth and marking the dawn of cultural and linguistic divides. This moment, whether taken as a historical event or a parable of human nature, offers a glimpse into the beginnings of a tribalism that thrives on division.

Other ancient traditions echo similar themes of division and the formation of distinct groups. Myths and legends from various cultures speak of gods, heroes, or natural forces that created boundaries between peoples, shaping their identities through language, geography, and custom. These stories, whether inscribed on stone tablets or passed down orally, suggest that the instinct to form tribes is as old as humanity itself. It is an instinct rooted in survival—a means of protecting resources, maintaining order, and ensuring continuity in a harsh and unpredictable world. Early tribes, defined by kinship and shared beliefs, were the foundation of communities. They provided belonging and security, but they also drew lines that separated friend from foe, insider from outsider.

This ancient tribalism was functional, even necessary, in a world where survival depended on cohesion. The shared identity of a tribe fostered cooperation, creating structures for governance, labor, and protection. Yet, it also sowed seeds of conflict. As tribes competed for resources or clashed over territory, their unity became a double-edged sword. The same strength that bonded individuals within a group often alienated or threatened those outside it. Tribalism became both a tool for survival and a catalyst for division.

As human societies grew, so did the complexity of their tribal structures. Tribes evolved into clans, city-states, and eventually nations, each with its own identity, language, and traditions. The early roots of tribalism expanded, weaving themselves into the fabric of civilizations. Yet, the underlying instinct remained unchanged. From the warring city-states of Mesopotamia to the formation of empires in Egypt and Rome, the drive to belong to a group—and to distinguish that group from others—shaped the course of history.

Even the earliest systems of law and governance reflect the influence of tribalism. Codes like Hammurabi's outlined justice within the context of a specific society, favoring those within the group while often excluding outsiders. Religious traditions also carried tribal markers, defining practices, taboos, and moral codes that strengthened group identity but often heightened division. In these early civilizations, tribalism was a lens through which the world was understood—a way of organizing reality into manageable parts, even as it laid the groundwork for conflict and exclusion.

The roots of tribalism, visible in these ancient narratives and systems, reveal an enduring aspect of human nature. It is an instinct that binds and protects, yet it also isolates and divides. The Tower of Babel and its echoes in other traditions offer not just a historical or mythological origin for this instinct, but a deeper insight into its dual nature. As the chapter unfolds, the ancient roots of tribalism set the stage for understanding how this force, born in the earliest days of humanity, continues to shape the modern world.

The Dawn of Division

The lands of the ancient world shaped the formation of tribes as much as the people themselves. Towering mountains stood as sentinels, isolating one group from another and giving birth to distinct cultures that flourished in their shadow. Rivers wound their way through fertile valleys, drawing communities to their banks while carving boundaries between them. Deserts, vast and unyielding, acted as both barriers and bridges, forcing tribes to adapt, to survive, and to define themselves against the harshness of nature. In every landscape, geography dictated the rhythms of life and the borders of belonging.

In these rugged terrains, survival was a daily struggle, and scarcity was often the rule. The need to secure food, water, and shelter forged a primal unity within tribes. In arid regions, where a single well could sustain a community, its ownership became a matter of life and death. Clashes over resources turned neighboring tribes into bitter rivals, their enmity growing as sharply as the stakes of survival. Geography did more than define the borders of territories; it etched the boundaries of identity, shaping how tribes saw themselves and their place in the world.

The environment's influence extended beyond survival. It molded culture, language, and even the stories that tribes told to explain their origins. In the steppes of Central Asia, the vast, open skies inspired myths of freedom and boundless possibility, while in the dense forests of Europe, tales often took on a more insular, guarded tone, reflecting the close confines of the trees. Geography was not just a backdrop; it was an active force, shaping the souls of those who lived within its bounds.

Tribalism, born from these geographical realities, was a response to the demands of life in an unforgiving world. It united people under a shared purpose, giving them the strength to endure hardships together. But as tribes grew stronger internally, their differences from others became more pronounced. The lines that defined their borders also divided their hearts, laying the groundwork for the conflicts that would echo through history.

The Power and Peril of Language

Language, the invisible thread that binds communities, played a central role in the formation of tribes. It was more than a tool for communication; it was the heartbeat of identity, a melody that resonated uniquely within each group. The Tower of Babel story speaks to this truth, illustrating how a shared tongue once unified humanity before its sudden fragmentation scattered them across the earth. With this divergence, language became not just a means of connection but also a barrier, creating divisions as profound as the geographical landscapes that separated tribes.

The rhythm and cadence of a tribe's speech held power. It whispered of shared stories, collective memories, and ancient traditions. Within the intimate circle of a tribe, language provided clarity and belonging, a sanctuary where every word was understood. But outside that circle, it became a wall. To encounter another tribe's tongue was to face the unfamiliar, a sound that alienated as much as it intrigued. Words that could unite within became tools of exclusion without, highlighting the invisible lines between "us" and "them."

As tribes evolved, their languages did too, shaped by their unique experiences and surroundings. A people dwelling in the shadow of mountains might develop words for every nuance of stone and slope, while those who lived by the sea spoke of tides and waves with a richness incomprehensible to those inland. Language rooted tribes in their environment, a living testament to their history and way of life. It was both a mirror reflecting their world and a shield guarding their identity.

Yet, this linguistic diversity came at a cost. Misunderstandings were inevitable when tribes encountered one another. Without a shared tongue, negotiations faltered, alliances wavered, and conflicts brewed. Language, so vital within a tribe, became a source of mistrust and division when tribes met. Even the simplest exchanges could spiral into hostility, driven by the inability to bridge the gap between two worlds.

The role of language in early tribalism reveals a profound duality. It was a force for cohesion, weaving individuals into a collective, yet it also deepened the divides between groups. In its evolution, language both connected and separated, embodying the essence of tribalism itself—a force that united within but fractured without.

Symbols of Identity

In the earliest days of tribal life, identity often took on visible, tangible forms. Symbols, more than mere decorations or tools, became the embodiment of a tribe's essence. Totems carved from wood, painted faces adorned with patterns of significance, and garments woven with distinctive colors all spoke of belonging. These symbols served as markers, declaring to the world who a tribe was, where it came from, and what it valued.

A painted shield displayed in battle was more than a defensive tool; it was a statement of pride and unity. The animal figures carved into its surface might evoke the spirit of a revered creature, believed to watch over the tribe and guide its fate. The songs sung around a fire carried melodies that, to outsiders, may have seemed incomprehensible but, to the tribe, resonated with generations of meaning. These artifacts and traditions transformed identity into something tangible, something that could be seen, heard, and felt.

Yet symbols were not just for the eyes of outsiders. Within the tribe, they reinforced solidarity and trust. When members donned the same patterns or invoked the same images, it was a reminder of their shared stories, struggles, and hopes. Symbols had the power to forge connections that were both emotional and practical, binding individuals together in a common purpose.

At the same time, these markers of identity often deepened the lines of separation. The very patterns that signified inclusion within a tribe highlighted exclusion to those outside it. A rival tribe's symbols could provoke fear, mistrust, or even anger, their meaning distorted by the lens of conflict. To stand out as "other" was to be set apart not just by appearance but by the full weight of a tribe's collective perception. The symbols of identity, while unifying within, became a form of visual and cultural language that divided without.

The significance of these early symbols extended far beyond their aesthetic value. They were the manifestations of belief, power, and belonging, a physical representation of the invisible bonds that held a tribe together. In every woven thread, carved figure, or spoken chant, symbols carried the weight of what it meant to belong—and what it meant to be set apart. Their legacy endures in the ways humans continue to use imagery, art, and rituals to define who they are, both individually and as part of something greater.

Conflict and Alliances

As tribes grew and spread across the landscapes of the ancient world, their interactions with one another became inevitable. These encounters, often fraught with tension, revealed the dual nature of tribalism. Tribes could form alliances, pooling their strength to face common threats, but they could also descend into conflict, competing for the same resources or seeking dominance over their neighbors. The boundaries between collaboration and rivalry were thin, often shifting with the winds of necessity and ambition.

Conflict was the most visible and destructive expression of tribalism. In a world where survival depended on access to fertile land, clean water, or safe hunting grounds, disputes over territory were not just matters of pride but of life and death. Rival tribes clashed over rivers and plains, each seeking to secure the means of their existence. The scars of these battles often lingered long after the fighting ceased, carried in the stories told around fires and etched into the memories of future generations.

At the same time, necessity could drive tribes to form alliances. When a larger threat loomed— whether from nature, such as a prolonged drought, or from a powerful enemy—tribes often found strength in unity. These alliances were pragmatic, built on mutual benefit rather than true trust. Still, they showcased the potential for cooperation even among groups with distinct identities and histories. Such collaborations often required tribes to put aside their differences, at least temporarily, for the sake of survival.

However, alliances were rarely simple or enduring. The same tribal instincts that fostered loyalty within a group often sowed seeds of distrust between groups. The fear of betrayal or the unequal division of resources could quickly unravel even the strongest partnerships. Tribes might come together to defeat a common enemy, only to find themselves at odds once the immediate danger had passed.

The patterns of conflict and alliance shaped the ancient world, leaving a legacy that continues to influence human behavior. These interactions reflected both the strengths and weaknesses of tribalism—its ability to unite and its propensity to divide. They revealed a fundamental truth about human nature: while unity could be achieved, it was often fleeting, overshadowed by the ever-present pull of self-preservation and group loyalty.

The story of tribalism's duality, seen in these cycles of conflict and cooperation, underscores its complexity. It is a force that has driven humanity to great achievements and devastating losses, a thread woven through the tapestry of history that still binds and divides to this day.

Parallel Narratives Across Cultures

The roots of tribalism stretch far beyond a single story or tradition. Across the ancient world, cultures wove their own narratives to explain the divisions and connections that defined human life. These myths and legends, though varied in their details, echo similar themes of identity, separation, and belonging, revealing the universality of tribal instincts.

In Greek mythology, the tale of Pandora's box captures the tension between unity and division. Pandora, the first woman created by the gods, opens a forbidden jar that unleashes chaos and suffering upon the world. What remains, however, is hope—a reminder of humanity's resilience even amid division. The story, like that of the Tower of Babel, speaks to a fall from harmony into fragmentation, where humanity is scattered and separated, yet still seeking connection and meaning.

Indigenous traditions also offer rich insights into the formation of tribes and their boundaries. Many Native American creation stories emphasize the sacred relationship between tribes and their environments. The land, often viewed as a living entity, becomes a central part of a tribe's identity. These stories reflect a deep connection to place, reinforcing a sense of belonging while defining the limits of "us" and "them." In these narratives, the natural world and human divisions are intertwined, shaping how tribes understand themselves and their role in the greater whole.

In the epic tales of Mesopotamia, such as the Epic of Gilgamesh, the tension between individual desires and collective identity is a recurring theme. Gilgamesh's journey reflects not only his quest for immortality but also his struggle to reconcile personal ambition with the responsibilities of leadership. These stories capture the essence of tribalism—how the needs of the many often stand in conflict with the aspirations of the few.

Each culture's narratives reveal how tribalism is both a unifying and dividing force. They provide a window into how ancient peoples understood their world and their place in it, offering lessons that still resonate. These stories remind us that tribalism is not bound by geography or time; it is a shared aspect of the human experience, a force that shapes identities and boundaries in ways both profound and enduring.

In these parallel narratives, the echoes of tribalism's origins ripple through history, demonstrating its impact across cultures and contexts. By examining these ancient stories, we gain a deeper understanding of the instincts that continue to influence human behavior, even in the modern age.

The Evolution of Leadership

As tribes formed and grew, leadership emerged as both a necessity and a defining characteristic. In the earliest days, leadership was often tied to survival—the strongest hunter, the wisest elder, or the most skilled healer naturally assumed positions of authority. These early leaders were not merely figureheads but embodiments of the tribe's values and goals. They guided their people through the uncertainties of life, making decisions that could mean the difference between thriving and perishing.

Leadership within a tribe was deeply personal. The bond between a leader and their people was forged in the fires of shared experience. A chief's authority might come from their ability to lead a successful hunt, their courage in battle, or their wisdom in resolving disputes. Yet, leadership was more than a practical role; it was a symbolic one. A leader represented the tribe's collective strength, serving as a living emblem of its identity and aspirations.

As tribes expanded, so did the complexity of leadership. In larger groups, authority often became stratified, with roles divided among those responsible for war, resource distribution, spiritual guidance, and governance. This evolution of leadership brought order to growing populations but also introduced new challenges. Power, once shared organically, began to consolidate, and with it came the potential for abuse and corruption.

The tension between loyalty and ambition often played out in the dynamics of tribal leadership. Stories from ancient cultures are rife with examples of leaders who rose to greatness only to falter under the weight of their power. The Mesopotamian king Gilgamesh, whose epic chronicles his journey from tyranny to wisdom, serves as a cautionary tale of how leadership can both unite and fracture a people. These narratives reflect the duality of leadership—its potential to guide tribes toward prosperity or plunge them into chaos.

Even within a cohesive tribe, the presence of a strong leader could ignite internal divisions. Ambition, envy, and disagreement over leadership styles or decisions sometimes fractured tribes from within. In such moments, tribalism's unifying power revealed its fragility, as loyalties shifted and groups splintered into factions. Leadership, while essential, was never immune to the pitfalls of human nature.

The evolution of leadership within tribes offers insight into the complexities of human organization. It highlights the delicate balance between unity and division, between guidance and control. Leadership was both a reflection of a tribe's identity and a force that shaped it, a dynamic that continues to influence the structures of power in modern societies. As tribes grew and changed, so too did the challenges and opportunities of leadership, leaving a legacy that echoes in the leaders of today.

The Psychology of Tribal Loyalty

Beneath the practical structures of tribal life lies a deeper force that binds individuals to their groups: the psychology of loyalty. This instinct, rooted in survival and social cohesion, is as ancient as humanity itself. To belong to a tribe was to ensure protection, identity, and purpose— a lifeline in a world fraught with uncertainty and danger.

Tribal loyalty was, at its core, a response to fear. The natural world presented countless threats, from predators lurking in the shadows to rival tribes encroaching on scarce resources. In such a world, isolation meant vulnerability, and unity meant strength. The bonds formed within a tribe provided not only safety but also a sense of control over an otherwise unpredictable existence. To stand with one's tribe was to stand against the chaos beyond its borders.

This loyalty was not purely rational; it was deeply emotional. The shared experiences of a tribe —celebrating victories, mourning losses, enduring hardships—fostered a sense of belonging that transcended individual concerns. Members of a tribe were not merely part of a group; they were part of a family, united by invisible threads of trust and mutual reliance. This bond was reinforced by rituals, traditions, and symbols that reminded individuals of their shared identity and purpose.

Yet, this loyalty came with a cost. The same instincts that fostered unity within a tribe often bred suspicion and hostility toward outsiders. The boundaries that defined "us" and "them" became psychological barriers, hardening perceptions and limiting empathy. Loyalty to the tribe could override moral considerations, leading individuals to justify actions that, under other circumstances, they might find unthinkable. The psychology of tribalism, while essential for cohesion, had a darker side—one that fueled conflict, prejudice, and exclusion.

The power of tribal loyalty lay in its ability to make individuals act against their self-interest for the sake of the group. A hunter might share his catch with the tribe, knowing it could mean going hungry himself. A warrior might risk his life to defend the community, driven not by personal gain but by the instinct to protect his people. These sacrifices, while noble, also revealed the depth of tribalism's grip on the human psyche—a force that could inspire both great acts of altruism and devastating acts of aggression.

The psychology of tribal loyalty offers a window into the human condition, revealing the tension between connection and division. It is a testament to the power of belonging, a force that has shaped humanity's journey from the earliest days of tribal life to the complexities of modern society. In understanding this instinct, we begin to see not only its enduring influence but also its potential to both unify and divide.

Tribalism and Human Evolution

The instinct to form tribes runs deeper than culture or tradition; it is woven into the fabric of human evolution. In the harsh environments of early humanity, survival demanded cooperation, and tribalism emerged as a natural strategy for ensuring collective success. It was not merely a choice but an evolutionary imperative, one that shaped how humans interacted, organized, and thrived.

Early humans faced a world where danger was ever-present. Predators prowled the shadows, resources were scarce, and the elements offered no mercy. Alone, an individual stood little chance against these threats. But within a group, the odds shifted. Together, people could pool their skills—one might excel at tracking prey, another at crafting tools, while yet another tended to the fire that kept the darkness at bay. The tribe became a living organism, its members functioning like interdependent cells, each playing a vital role in its survival.

This interdependence bred loyalty and trust, traits that were not only advantageous but essential. The individuals who thrived were those who could bond with others, forming alliances and building networks of mutual support. Over generations, these traits were passed down, hardwired into the human brain. The drive to belong, to protect one's group, and to see outsiders with caution or suspicion became evolutionary adaptations, tools for navigating a dangerous and unpredictable world.

But evolution's gifts often come with a cost. The same instincts that helped early tribes flourish also sowed the seeds of conflict. Tribalism encouraged competition, not just within a group but also between groups. The desire to secure resources, assert dominance, or protect territory led to clashes that shaped the course of human history. While cooperation within a tribe was vital, competition with other tribes could be just as fierce. This duality—cooperation and conflict— became a defining feature of humanity's evolutionary journey.

Tribalism also influenced how humans viewed the world and each other. The brain, attuned to recognizing patterns and categorizing information, naturally extended this ability to social interactions. Members of the tribe were seen as allies, while those outside it were viewed as potential threats. This tendency to divide the world into "us" and "them" was not born of malice but of survival—a mechanism that ensured caution in uncertain encounters. Yet, it also limited the capacity for empathy and understanding, creating barriers that persist even in modern societies.

As humanity evolved, so too did its tribes. What began as small, kin-based groups expanded into larger and more complex societies. Yet, the tribal instincts that had once ensured survival remained, shaping behaviors and systems in ways that continue to resonate. From the boardrooms of corporations to the voting booths of democracies, the echoes of early tribalism still influence decisions, loyalties, and conflicts.

Tribalism's role in human evolution is both a testament to its power and a cautionary tale. It highlights how deeply this instinct is embedded in who we are, offering insight into why we act as we do and why overcoming division requires conscious effort. In understanding its origins, we gain a clearer view of its impact—a force that has carried humanity forward while always threatening to pull it apart.

Tribalism's Enduring Legacy

The roots of tribalism, planted deep in humanity's earliest days, have grown into a legacy that continues to shape the modern world. While the tribal structures of ancient times have largely dissolved, their influence lingers in the ways humans organize, identify, and interact. Tribes may no longer be defined by shared geography or immediate survival needs, but their spirit persists in the groups and affiliations that dominate contemporary life.

The systems of governance, law, and community that define civilizations owe much to tribal origins. Early codes like Hammurabi's, which established justice and societal order, reflect the tribal instinct to protect the group while delineating insiders from outsiders. These systems, designed to promote harmony within, often did so at the expense of those beyond their reach. The sense of belonging they fostered carried with it the implicit exclusion of those who did not share the same identity, language, or beliefs.

Even as societies expanded and evolved, tribal instincts remained embedded in their foundations. Nations emerged as macro-tribes, their boundaries drawn by shared language, culture, or ideology. The conflicts that shaped the rise and fall of empires were fueled by the same forces that once drove disputes over a single watering hole. The scale may have grown, but the underlying dynamic—the competition for resources, power, and identity—remained unchanged.

In the modern era, tribalism has found new expressions. Political parties, social movements, and even fandoms serve as contemporary tribes, offering a sense of belonging in an increasingly complex world. These affiliations provide identity and purpose, echoing the roles of ancient tribes, yet they also perpetuate division. The same forces that unify individuals within these groups often alienate those who stand outside them, deepening the divides between "us" and "them."

The legacy of tribalism is also evident in how humans perceive and respond to threats. The instinct to protect one's group, once vital for survival, now manifests in behaviors that can hinder collaboration and understanding. Whether in international diplomacy or local disputes, the tendency to prioritize the interests of one's own tribe often eclipses the broader goal of unity and progress.

Tribalism's endurance is a testament to its deep roots in human nature, but it also presents a challenge. To navigate its influence requires an awareness of its power and a willingness to confront its darker aspects. By understanding its legacy, humanity can begin to transcend its divisions, drawing on the strengths of tribalism—cohesion, loyalty, and identity—while striving to overcome its limitations. The echoes of ancient tribes remain, shaping the present and offering lessons for the future, reminding us that the path forward lies in balancing the ties that bind with the bridges that unite.

The Path Forward

The enduring presence of tribalism in human history underscores its dual nature as both a source of strength and a cause of division. While its roots lie in survival and identity, its modern manifestations often challenge humanity's ability to live harmoniously in an interconnected world. Understanding these roots is only the beginning; the true challenge lies in finding a path forward, one that embraces the positive aspects of tribalism while mitigating its harmful effects.

At its best, tribalism fosters unity and purpose. It gives individuals a sense of belonging and shared identity, creating communities that can support and uplift. This instinct, honed over millennia, can still serve humanity, provided it is directed toward inclusive rather than exclusive goals. To move forward, societies must learn to channel this instinct in ways that build connections across divides rather than deepen them.

Education and awareness play a critical role in this process. By understanding the psychological and historical foundations of tribalism, individuals can begin to recognize its influence on their own behaviors and decisions. This awareness allows for a more intentional approach to relationships, where empathy and dialogue replace assumptions and prejudice. The ability to see others not as members of an opposing tribe but as fellow humans with shared goals and challenges is a crucial step toward progress.

Technology, though often a catalyst for modern tribalism, can also be a tool for overcoming it. While algorithms may amplify division, they also have the potential to foster connection. Platforms that encourage diverse perspectives and facilitate meaningful interactions can help bridge the gaps that tribalism creates. The challenge lies in using technology to unite rather than isolate, to build communities that reflect the interconnected reality of the modern world.

Leadership is another pivotal factor in transcending tribalism. Leaders who prioritize collaboration over competition, who seek common ground rather than division, can set an example for their communities. By fostering environments where diverse perspectives are valued and differences are seen as strengths, leaders can help redefine what it means to belong.

Ultimately, the path forward requires a reimagining of tribalism itself. It is not about erasing identity or suppressing the instinct to belong but about expanding the boundaries of what constitutes a tribe. When humanity learns to see itself as a single, interconnected community, the potential for progress becomes boundless. The legacy of tribalism, with all its complexities, offers a roadmap—not just a history of division, but a guide to understanding how unity might be achieved. In this reimagining, the ties that once bound small groups can become the threads that weave together a global tapestry of shared purpose and connection.

Beyond the Tribal Instinct

Tribalism, though ancient in its origins, remains a defining force in the modern world. Its legacy can be seen in the nations we build, the communities we cherish, and the conflicts that divide us. It is a paradoxical force, both a source of strength and a seed of discord, capable of uniting people under shared identities while fracturing humanity into opposing camps.

The instinct to belong is deeply ingrained, a survival mechanism that has shaped the course of human evolution and the structure of societies. Yet, the same instinct that once ensured survival now threatens progress. The lines we draw—between races, religions, political ideologies, and nations—may have evolved from ancient tribal boundaries, but their impact is no less profound. These divisions often obscure the shared humanity that connects us all, perpetuating cycles of misunderstanding, conflict, and exclusion.

Moving beyond tribalism does not mean abandoning the desire to belong. Rather, it calls for a redefinition of what belonging means. It challenges us to expand our tribes, to see others not as outsiders but as part of a greater whole. This shift requires a conscious effort to confront the biases and fears that tribalism fosters, replacing them with empathy, understanding, and a commitment to unity.

The journey beyond the tribal instinct is not an easy one. It demands a willingness to question assumptions, to engage with perspectives different from our own, and to embrace the complexity of human relationships. It calls for leadership that inspires and unites, technology that connects rather than isolates, and education that fosters critical thinking and compassion.

As humanity faces the challenges of an interconnected world, the lessons of tribalism offer both caution and hope. They remind us of the power of belonging and the dangers of division, of the bonds that tie us together and the walls that keep us apart. In understanding these lessons, we can begin to chart a new course—one that honors the strengths of our tribal past while striving for a future defined by unity and shared purpose.

In this effort, the legacy of tribalism becomes more than a history of division; it becomes a blueprint for building a world where belonging is not limited by the boundaries of tribe but extended to all. Beyond the tribal instinct lies the potential for something greater—a humanity that recognizes its differences not as barriers but as the foundation for connection and growth.

Cultural Case Studies

Across the ancient world, the pulse of tribalism shaped civilizations in unique and enduring ways. In the arid deserts of the Middle East, nomadic tribes roamed the vast expanses, their lives woven into the rhythms of the sands and stars. These tribes, bound by kinship and shared struggle, often clashed with the more settled peoples who cultivated the fertile lands of the river valleys. The tension between these two ways of life—one transient and the other rooted— sparked cycles of conflict and cooperation. Trade routes became lifelines where goods and ideas flowed, yet these same paths were often battlegrounds, their dust marked by the struggle for dominance and survival.

The Greek city-states, perched along rocky coasts and nestled in lush valleys, offer another vivid tapestry of tribalism at work. Each city-state, or polis, functioned as its own tribe, fiercely proud of its autonomy and identity. Athens championed philosophy and democracy, its citizens gathering in bustling forums to debate the nature of justice and truth. Sparta, by contrast, glorified discipline and military might, its warriors embodying the unyielding strength of their people. While these city-states shared language, religion, and heritage, their rivalries often overshadowed their commonalities. The Peloponnesian War, a brutal conflict between Athens and Sparta, exemplifies how tribalism's unifying power within could fuel devastating divisions without.

Further east, the ancient Silk Road threaded its way through deserts and mountains, connecting tribes and cultures across continents. Here, tribalism took on a more complex form. Nomadic groups like the Scythians and Sogdians became intermediaries, bridging the divide between empires through trade and diplomacy. These tribes carried silk and spices, but also stories, technologies, and beliefs, weaving a rich tapestry of cultural exchange. Yet, even amidst this connectivity, the boundaries of identity remained firm. The same routes that brought cooperation also carried conflict, as tribes vied for control of the precious lifelines that sustained their way of life.

In sub-Saharan Africa, tribalism manifested in intricate systems of governance and kinship. The Bantu migrations, a sweeping movement of peoples over centuries, spread language, agriculture, and ironworking across vast regions. Tribal identities were preserved through oral traditions, their histories sung and spoken by griots who carried the weight of generations in their words. These migrations exemplified the fluidity of tribalism—how it could adapt, expand, and yet remain rooted in the shared memories and values of its people.

Each of these case studies reflects the dual nature of tribalism. It was a force for unity, forging bonds within groups and creating systems that sustained life and culture. Yet it also sowed division, as the instinct to protect and prioritize one's tribe often led to tension and conflict. The stories of these ancient peoples reveal not only the resilience of tribalism but also its enduring challenges, echoing patterns that still shape the world today.

Tribalism and Religion

The intertwining of tribalism and religion is as ancient as humanity itself. In the earliest tribes, belief systems were deeply tied to their identity, serving as both a spiritual compass and a social framework. Gods were often seen as protectors of the tribe, intimately connected to their land, their struggles, and their victories. Worship was not just an individual act but a communal one, reinforcing the bonds that held the tribe together.

In Mesopotamia, each city-state had its patron deity, a god or goddess believed to watch over its people and ensure their prosperity. The towering ziggurats of Ur and Babylon were not merely architectural marvels but declarations of tribal identity and divine favor. To honor these deities was to affirm one's place within the community, to strengthen the invisible threads that tied individuals to one another and to their shared history.

Elsewhere, tribal religions took on forms that were inseparable from their environment. In Indigenous cultures around the world, spiritual practices often revolved around the land and its cycles. Mountains, rivers, and animals were imbued with sacred significance, their spirits woven into the fabric of daily life. These beliefs did more than connect tribes to the natural world; they distinguished one group from another, as each tribe's myths and rituals reflected its unique relationship with its surroundings.

Religious leaders, whether shamans, priests, or prophets, held pivotal roles within these early tribes. They were seen as intermediaries between the mortal and the divine, their words and actions shaping the moral and social codes of their communities. Their authority reinforced the tribe's unity, offering guidance and resolve in times of uncertainty. Yet, the power of religion to unite within also heightened divisions without. Conflicts often arose when the gods of one tribe were pitted against those of another, their followers believing their own deities to be superior or their rituals more righteous.

The exclusivity of tribal religions often mirrored the exclusivity of tribalism itself. Worship was tied to membership, and to worship another tribe's gods was to risk alienation—or worse, betrayal. This exclusivity reinforced tribal boundaries, creating a spiritual line between "us" and "them" that deepened social and cultural divides. In some cases, these boundaries erupted into violence, as religious identity became yet another front in the ongoing competition for survival and dominance.

Despite its divisive potential, religion also served as a source of profound meaning and resilience. It gave tribes a sense of purpose, offering narratives that explained their origins, justified their struggles, and promised hope for the future. These narratives, passed down through generations, preserved the essence of the tribe even as external pressures threatened to erase it. The interplay between tribalism and religion is a testament to their shared power: both are forces that connect and divide, that define and exclude, shaping the story of humanity in ways that endure to this day.

Art and Storytelling

Long before the written word, art and storytelling were the primary means by which tribes preserved their identity and passed down their collective wisdom. Every stroke of paint on a cave wall, every tale told under the glow of a fire, carried the weight of history and meaning. These creative expressions were not just cultural adornments but vital tools for survival, unity, and distinction. They helped tribes make sense of their world, reinforce their bonds, and define themselves against others.

In the shadowy depths of caves like those in Lascaux and Altamira, early humans left behind vivid depictions of animals, hunts, and symbols. These images were more than artistic endeavors; they were declarations of identity and connection to the natural world. Each scene told a story, a shared memory etched into stone that bound the tribe together. These paintings likely held spiritual significance as well, invoking the favor of gods or spirits for successful hunts and safe journeys.

Storytelling was equally vital, giving voice to the values, fears, and aspirations of a tribe. Around flickering campfires, elders recounted tales of creation, heroes, and ancestral triumphs. These stories served as both entertainment and education, teaching younger generations the lessons of their forebears. Through oral traditions, tribes preserved their knowledge of the land, their laws, and their place in the cosmos. Every tale was a thread in the fabric of their identity, woven tightly into the collective memory of the tribe.

Art and storytelling also marked the boundaries between tribes. The symbols painted on shields or etched into pottery distinguished one group from another, serving as both a warning and a declaration of pride. Stories often contained subtle—or explicit—messages about the superiority of the tribe's customs or the inferiority of others'. These cultural markers reinforced tribal cohesion while heightening the sense of "us" versus "them."

Yet, these creative expressions were not merely divisive. They also acted as bridges, providing a means for tribes to share ideas and build connections. When trade routes brought different tribes into contact, their art and stories often traveled alongside their goods. A carved artifact or a borrowed tale could transcend tribal boundaries, sparking moments of understanding and exchange even amidst tension.

Art and storytelling encapsulated the essence of tribalism: the need to define oneself, to belong, and to endure. They were tools of preservation and distinction, instruments of unity and division. The creativity of these early tribes left an indelible mark on humanity, reminding us that even in a world marked by competition and conflict, the drive to express, to communicate, and to connect is universal. These early expressions laid the foundation for the art and narratives that continue to shape human culture today.

From Tribes to Nations

As tribes expanded and evolved, the seeds of larger societies began to take root. What started as small, tightly knit groups bound by kinship and necessity gradually grew into sprawling networks of city-states, kingdoms, and nations. This transition was not a simple progression but a complex, often tumultuous process marked by both opportunities and tensions. Tribal identities, once defined by proximity and shared struggle, were challenged and reshaped by the demands of larger, more diverse communities.

In Mesopotamia, the cradle of civilization, the first city-states rose from the fertile plains between the Tigris and Euphrates rivers. Tribes that once roamed these lands began to settle, drawn together by the promise of agricultural abundance. Cities like Uruk and Eridu became hubs of culture and commerce, their towering ziggurats standing as symbols of collective achievement. Yet, even within these burgeoning urban centers, the remnants of tribalism persisted. Neighborhoods were often divided along familial or ethnic lines, and allegiances to one's clan or tribe remained powerful forces, sometimes undermining the broader unity of the city-state.

The formation of nations brought even greater complexity. As rulers consolidated power, they sought to unify disparate tribes under a single banner. This unification was often achieved through shared language, religion, or law—tools that created a sense of collective identity. Hammurabi's Code, one of history's earliest legal systems, exemplifies this effort. Its detailed regulations sought to impose order on a diverse population, ensuring fairness within the group while reinforcing loyalty to the state. Yet, this cohesion came at a cost, as those outside the nation's boundaries were often excluded or viewed as adversaries.

The rise of empires magnified these dynamics. Leaders like Alexander the Great and the emperors of Rome sought to integrate vast territories under their rule, blending cultures and traditions while maintaining control. This process of assimilation required a delicate balance, as the loyalty of conquered tribes had to be secured without erasing their identities entirely. Imperial systems often relied on a combination of force and diplomacy, using tribal leaders as intermediaries to manage their people. The result was a patchwork of unity and division, where the pull of tribal loyalty continued to compete with the larger political structure.

Despite these challenges, the transition from tribes to nations brought remarkable achievements. It allowed for the development of shared infrastructure, such as roads and aqueducts, that connected once-isolated communities. It fostered innovations in governance, philosophy, and art, as diverse perspectives came into contact and sparked new ideas. Yet, the echoes of tribalism never disappeared. Even as societies grew larger and more interconnected, the instinct to prioritize one's group remained a defining characteristic of human behavior.

The journey from tribes to nations is a testament to humanity's ability to adapt and organize on a grand scale. It reflects the enduring influence of tribalism, both as a source of strength and as a challenge to unity. This transition laid the groundwork for the modern world, where the tensions between local identity and global belonging continue to shape societies in profound ways. The evolution of human organization, from small tribes to sprawling nations, demonstrates the complexity of our shared history and the resilience of the tribal instinct that lies at its core.

Foreshadowing the Modern Connection

The echoes of tribalism reverberate throughout human history, but they are not confined to the past. The instincts and patterns that shaped ancient tribes continue to manifest in the modern world, albeit in transformed and often disguised forms. From political affiliations to digital communities, the tribal tendencies that once ensured survival now influence everything from personal identities to global conflicts. Understanding this continuity requires bridging the gap between the ancient and the modern, tracing the threads of tribalism as they weave through time.

The lines drawn between ancient tribes find their counterparts in today's national borders, ideological divides, and cultural identities. Just as early tribes competed for resources and territory, modern nations and corporations vie for influence and power on the global stage. The competition remains fierce, though the tools of engagement—diplomacy, trade, technology, and war—have evolved. The instinct to protect and prioritize one's group, so vital in the past, still shapes decisions and policies in profound ways.

Even in interpersonal relationships, the tribal instinct persists. Social groups, clubs, and even workplaces often mimic the dynamics of ancient tribes, fostering a sense of belonging while delineating insiders and outsiders. The rapid rise of digital platforms has amplified these tendencies, creating virtual tribes that form around shared interests, ideologies, or goals. These digital communities, while offering connection and identity, also heighten polarization, echoing the same patterns of unity within and division without that defined ancient tribes.

The legacy of tribalism is also evident in the human response to crises. Natural disasters, pandemics, and geopolitical upheavals often reveal the strength—and the limits—of collective action. In moments of uncertainty, people tend to retreat into the safety of their tribes, whether defined by family, community, or ideology. While this instinct can provide comfort and solidarity, it can also hinder broader cooperation, as tribal loyalties clash with the need for unified responses.

The connection between ancient and modern tribalism is not merely a matter of historical curiosity; it is a lens through which to view the challenges and opportunities of contemporary life. By recognizing the parallels between the past and the present, we gain insight into the forces that shape our world and the decisions we make. This understanding offers a foundation for addressing the divisions that persist, allowing us to navigate the complexities of modern society with greater clarity and intention.

The journey through the ancient roots of tribalism reveals patterns that continue to define humanity. As the narrative transitions to the modern era, the enduring influence of these ancient instincts becomes clear. The lessons of the past serve not only as a reflection but as a guide, illuminating the ways tribalism has adapted to new contexts and challenges. This continuity underscores the relevance of tribalism in understanding the human experience, offering a bridge between history and the present, and paving the way for a deeper exploration of its modern manifestations.

Reflection on the Ancient Roots of Tribalism

From its inception in the first scattered tribes to its echoes in the formation of nations and cultures, tribalism has been both a guide and a challenge for humanity. It has nurtured bonds of kinship and solidarity, preserving identity and purpose in the face of uncertainty. Yet, it has also drawn lines of exclusion, fostering rivalries that have shaped the course of history. The patterns of tribalism, born in the ancient world, remain deeply embedded in human nature, influencing not only how societies evolved but how they continue to function today. As we move from the shadows of antiquity into the complexities of the modern era, these ancient instincts will reveal their enduring hold on humanity, guiding us to confront both their power and their peril.

A Drive to Belong

The human heart has always yearned for connection, an unspoken longing as natural as the air we breathe. In the vastness of an unpredictable world, the desire to belong has served as both anchor and compass, guiding individuals toward the safety of shared identity and purpose. To belong is to be seen, to be valued, to find one's place in a collective story—a need so profound it has shaped decisions, relationships, and the course of history itself.

In ancient times, the need for connection was inseparable from survival. A lone wanderer could scarcely hope to endure the perils of the natural world, but within a tribe, there was strength in numbers. Each member of the group played a role, their contributions weaving a tapestry of mutual reliance and shared destiny. The hunter who risked the wilderness, the healer who soothed wounds, the elder who carried the wisdom of generations—all were bound by invisible threads of loyalty and trust. Belonging was more than a privilege; it was a necessity.

This primal drive did more than ensure survival; it shaped identity. A person was not merely an individual but part of a living whole. The tribe's triumphs and losses became their own, the stories of the past echoing in their present. It was within the tribe that individuals discovered who they were and what they stood for, their sense of self defined by the rhythms and rituals of their group. This shared identity offered comfort, a balm for the uncertainties of life, yet it also demanded a price.

Belonging often required conformity. To challenge the tribe's customs or question its decisions was to risk exclusion, a fate as terrifying as death itself in the ancient world. The same bonds that united the tribe could entangle the individual, leaving no room for dissent or divergence. The loyalty that protected and uplifted could also blind, narrowing perceptions and fostering judgment. Within these tensions lay the seeds of both betrayal and resilience, as those who stepped outside the tribe's bounds found themselves at odds with the very community that had once defined them.

The allure of belonging is as powerful today as it was millennia ago. Modern tribes take many forms—families, friendships, workplaces, political affiliations, and digital communities—all echoing the dynamics of their ancient predecessors. These groups offer identity and purpose, binding people together in shared goals and values. Yet, like the tribes of old, they also draw lines, dividing "us" from "them" and leaving little room for understanding those outside their fold.

Stories of loyalty and betrayal reveal the complexities of this drive. History is replete with tales of individuals who stood by their tribes in times of hardship, sacrificing personal gain for the good of the group. It is equally marked by the pain of exclusion—of those cast out for challenging the status quo or daring to follow a different path. These narratives speak to the dual nature of belonging, a force that can both uplift and constrain.

The tension between inclusion and exclusion remains an enduring theme in the human experience. To belong is to find connection and identity, but it is also to navigate the boundaries of loyalty and independence. The psychology of this drive shapes not only how we see ourselves but also how we relate to one another, reinforcing the patterns of tribalism that continue to influence the modern world. As this chapter unfolds, it offers a deeper exploration of the allure and complexity of belonging, illuminating the ways in which this primal instinct defines, divides, and unites us all.

The Allure of Inclusion

Inclusion offers a warmth that is both irresistible and deeply comforting, like the glow of a fire on a cold night. To be included is to feel seen, valued, and understood, a sensation that strikes at the core of what it means to be human. This allure is no accident; it is the product of centuries of evolution, where inclusion within a group ensured survival and strengthened bonds. It is why a word of affirmation or an act of acceptance can resonate so profoundly—it taps into an ancient, almost instinctive need to belong.

For early humans, inclusion was more than an emotional comfort; it was a matter of life and death. To be accepted within a tribe meant access to shared resources, protection from predators, and the security of a communal identity. These benefits were tangible and immediate, and they fostered a sense of trust and solidarity that held tribes together. Inclusion also provided a framework for understanding the world. Within the safety of the tribe, individuals could make sense of their experiences, guided by shared stories, rituals, and customs.

But the pull of inclusion is not purely practical. It also shapes how individuals see themselves. To be included is to have a role, to know one's place in the intricate web of relationships that make up a community. This sense of identity is powerful, offering both stability and purpose. It reassures individuals that they are part of something larger than themselves, connected by bonds that transcend their own existence. It is a feeling of home, a tether to meaning in an otherwise chaotic world.

Yet, the allure of inclusion often blinds as much as it comforts. The desire to remain within a group can lead individuals to silence their doubts, suppress their individuality, or turn a blind eye to injustices perpetuated by the tribe. Loyalty to the group can eclipse loyalty to truth or personal integrity, creating a moral gray area where inclusion becomes a double-edged sword. The same acceptance that offers solace can demand conformity, leaving those who dare to question or challenge on the outside looking in.

This tension has played out across history, from ancient tribes to modern movements. The stories of those who sacrificed everything for the sake of belonging, and those who were excluded for refusing to conform, reveal the complexity of this dynamic. Inclusion is both a gift and a burden, a force that unites and divides, heals and harms.

The allure of inclusion, though rooted in the survival instincts of ancient tribes, continues to shape human behavior in profound ways. It influences decisions, relationships, and even the way societies are structured. As humanity evolves, the question remains: how can we embrace the comfort of inclusion without succumbing to its pitfalls? The answer lies in understanding not only what inclusion gives but also what it asks of us, illuminating a path forward that honors the beauty of connection while acknowledging its complexities.

The Cost of Exclusion

If inclusion is the warmth of the fire, exclusion is the chill of the wilderness beyond its glow. To be cast out, whether by choice or force, is to face a profound loss—of safety, identity, and connection. For early humans, exclusion from the tribe was often synonymous with death. Without the protection of the group, the lone individual was left vulnerable to predators, starvation, and the unforgiving forces of nature. Yet, the sting of exclusion is not only physical; it is deeply emotional, a wound that cuts into the very fabric of one's sense of self.

The cost of exclusion has always been steep. In the ancient world, tribes functioned as both social and survival units. To be part of a tribe meant access to its resources, stories, and traditions. It meant a role, a purpose, and a sense of belonging. Exclusion severed these ties, leaving the individual adrift. The rituals that once provided comfort became inaccessible, the voices of the tribe replaced by silence. Exclusion was more than isolation—it was an erasure, a denial of one's place in the communal narrative.

Exclusion also carried with it a stigma that could ripple far beyond the individual. To be cast out was to be marked, a cautionary tale for others within the tribe. Those who remained were reminded of the cost of dissent or failure to conform. The tribe's unity was maintained, but at the expense of the outcast, whose exile served as both punishment and warning. The fear of exclusion, then, became a powerful force, driving individuals to align themselves more closely with the group, often at the cost of their own values or identity.

This tension—the pull of inclusion and the fear of exclusion—has defined human behavior for millennia. Even in modern society, where physical survival is less dependent on group membership, the emotional and psychological costs of exclusion remain significant. To be left out, ignored, or rejected can lead to feelings of shame, alienation, and a loss of self-worth. Social exclusion is not merely a personal experience; it is a societal dynamic, shaping how groups maintain cohesion and enforce norms.

Exclusion also exposes the darker side of tribalism. While belonging fosters connection and solidarity within a group, it often does so by creating boundaries that define who is in and who is out. These boundaries, though invisible, are deeply felt, reinforcing the divisions that keep humanity apart. The cost of exclusion, then, is not only borne by the individual but by society as a whole, as the lines drawn by tribalism hinder unity and understanding.

The stories of exclusion—of those who dared to challenge their tribe, of those cast out for being different, of those who walked away to find their own path—reveal the profound impact of this dynamic. They remind us that while tribalism has the power to protect and uplift, it also has the potential to isolate and wound. To understand the cost of exclusion is to confront the limits of belonging and to grapple with the complexities of human connection, a tension that remains as relevant today as it was in the tribal fires of long ago.

The Psychology of Belonging

The human mind is intricately wired for connection, a tapestry of neural pathways that respond to social cues with profound sensitivity. Neuroscience reveals that the same regions of the brain activated by physical pain are also engaged when we experience social rejection. This overlap underscores how deeply the need to belong is embedded within our very being. It is not merely a social construct but a fundamental aspect of our psychology, driving behaviors and influencing decisions often beyond our conscious awareness.

From infancy, attachment shapes our understanding of the world. A child's bond with caregivers forms the foundation for future relationships, instilling patterns of trust, empathy, and cooperation. These early connections teach us that others can provide comfort, safety, and affirmation, reinforcing the instinct to seek out and maintain social bonds. As we grow, this desire for affiliation extends beyond family to friends, communities, and larger social groups, each offering a sense of identity and belonging.

Psychologists have long studied this intrinsic motivation, identifying it as a core human need alongside food and shelter. Theories such as Maslow's hierarchy of needs place belongingness just above physiological and safety needs, highlighting its crucial role in overall well-being. When this need is met, individuals tend to exhibit higher self-esteem, better mental health, and increased resilience. Conversely, a lack of belonging can lead to loneliness, anxiety, and a host of other psychological challenges.

The drive to belong also influences group dynamics and societal structures. Social Identity Theory suggests that individuals derive a significant part of their self-concept from the groups to which they belong. This identification fosters in-group favoritism, where loyalty and preference are given to one's own group, sometimes at the expense of others. While this can strengthen cohesion within the group, it can also lead to prejudice and discrimination against those perceived as outsiders.

Cognitive biases further illustrate how the psychology of belonging affects perception and judgment. The confirmation bias, for instance, leads individuals to seek out information that reinforces their existing beliefs and affiliations, ignoring or dismissing contradictory evidence. This mental shortcut can deepen divisions and hinder open-mindedness, as people become entrenched in their viewpoints, aligned with their chosen groups.

The allure of echo chambers, both in personal interactions and through media consumption, stems from this psychological inclination. Surrounding oneself with like-minded individuals and information creates a comforting environment where beliefs are validated, and challenges are minimized. While this can enhance a sense of belonging, it also narrows perspectives, limiting growth and understanding.

In modern society, the psychology of belonging manifests in various ways, from the camaraderie of sports fans to the solidarity of social movements. It drives trends, shapes cultures, and influences everything from consumer behavior to political affiliations. Marketers, politicians, and leaders often tap into this need, crafting messages that resonate with group identities and values, knowing that the desire to belong can be a powerful motivator.

Understanding the psychology of belonging offers insight into both the potential and the pitfalls of tribalism. It reveals why individuals may cling to groups even when it goes against their self-interest or moral compass, and why breaking free from harmful affiliations can be so challenging. Recognizing these patterns empowers individuals to reflect on their own motivations and to seek connections that are healthy, inclusive, and aligned with their true values.

As we navigate the complexities of human relationships and societal structures, the psychology of belonging remains a central theme. It is a force that can unite or divide, heal or harm, depending on how it is understood and channeled. By exploring this intricate aspect of our nature, we gain the tools to foster connections that enrich our lives and contribute to a more empathetic and cohesive society.

Stories of Loyalty and Betrayal

Throughout history, the tension between loyalty and betrayal has played out in countless narratives, reflecting the profound complexities of belonging. Loyalty is a bond rooted in trust, shared values, and mutual reliance—a force that unites and defines groups. Yet, when that trust is broken, when the boundaries of belonging are challenged, betrayal emerges as its stark opposite, tearing at the very fabric of relationships and communities. These dual forces are deeply entwined with the human experience, illuminating both the strength and fragility of tribal ties.

In ancient tribes, loyalty was often a matter of survival. To stand with one's people, to defend the group against external threats, was a sacred duty. Stories of heroism and sacrifice were passed down through generations, extolling those who placed the needs of the tribe above their own. These tales served not only to inspire but to reinforce the values and expectations that bound individuals to the collective. A hunter who shared his kill or a warrior who defended the tribe embodied the ideals of loyalty, ensuring the survival of the group and earning a revered place in its narrative.

Betrayal, by contrast, was seen as the ultimate transgression. To act against the tribe, whether by breaking its rules, aiding its enemies, or abandoning it in times of need, was to sever the trust that held the group together. Such acts were often met with severe consequences—exile, punishment, or even death—not merely as retribution but as a means of preserving the tribe's unity. The stories of those who betrayed their people were cautionary tales, their names remembered with shame and their actions condemned as warnings to others.

These dynamics are not confined to the past. In modern contexts, loyalty and betrayal continue to shape relationships and communities. Families, friendships, organizations, and nations all rely on trust to function, and the breach of that trust can have devastating effects. Political movements splinter when factions feel betrayed by their leaders; companies crumble when employees act against their organization; even close personal bonds can be irreparably damaged when loyalty falters.

The interplay between loyalty and betrayal also reveals the complexity of moral choice. Loyalty can sometimes demand actions that conflict with broader ethical principles, placing individuals in difficult positions. Betrayal, though often seen as wholly negative, can sometimes be an act of courage—choosing to stand against the harmful actions of a group for the sake of a greater good. These moral ambiguities highlight the tension inherent in belonging, where the boundaries of right and wrong are not always clear.

The stories of loyalty and betrayal, whether drawn from ancient legends or modern events, underscore the profound influence of tribalism on human behavior. They remind us that belonging is not a static state but a dynamic interplay of trust, expectation, and choice. By examining these narratives, we gain insight into the forces that bind us together and the fractures that threaten to pull us apart, shedding light on the enduring complexities of the human condition.

The Tension Between Inclusion and Exclusion

The intricate dance between inclusion and exclusion is a defining characteristic of tribalism, shaping how groups form, function, and endure. To be included is to feel the warmth of acceptance, to know that one's presence matters within a collective. Exclusion, on the other hand, is its cold shadow, a reminder of boundaries that separate "us" from "them." This tension is as old as humanity itself, rooted in the instinct to protect and preserve the group while warding off perceived threats.

Inclusion creates bonds that are vital for cohesion. It fosters trust and shared identity, reinforcing the sense that members of a group are not just individuals but parts of a whole. Within the safety of inclusion, people find validation and purpose, their roles and contributions acknowledged and celebrated. This dynamic strengthens not only the individual but also the collective, as unity often translates to resilience in the face of external challenges.

Yet inclusion, by its very nature, demands exclusion. To define who belongs, a group must also decide who does not. These boundaries, though intangible, carry immense power. They delineate insiders from outsiders, shaping perceptions and influencing behaviors. While inclusion binds individuals together, exclusion separates them, often reinforcing stereotypes, mistrust, and conflict. The lines drawn by tribalism are rarely neutral; they are imbued with the weight of history, culture, and emotion, deepening divisions that can persist for generations.

The tension between these forces is not limited to ancient tribes or historical conflicts. It plays out in modern contexts with startling regularity. A workplace team might celebrate its camaraderie while subtly ostracizing a colleague who challenges the status quo. A political movement might rally around shared ideals while vilifying those who question its methods. Even social media, with its promise of connection, often amplifies this tension, creating echo chambers that exclude dissenting voices while reinforcing groupthink.

This dynamic also has a profound impact on identity. For those included, the sense of belonging can be empowering, affirming their place in the world. For those excluded, the experience can be isolating and disorienting, leading to feelings of alienation and resentment. The pain of exclusion often lingers, shaping how individuals view themselves and others, while the comfort of inclusion can blind groups to the harm they may cause to those on the outside.

The stories of inclusion and exclusion reveal the dual nature of tribalism: its ability to unite and its propensity to divide. They show how the same mechanisms that foster connection can also create barriers, leaving humanity caught in a perpetual balancing act. Understanding this tension is crucial, not only for navigating relationships and communities but also for addressing the broader societal challenges that stem from tribal instincts. As the boundaries between "us" and "them" continue to evolve, the challenge remains to embrace the strength of inclusion without succumbing to the pitfalls of exclusion, fostering unity that is both meaningful and just.

The Fragility of Belonging

Belonging, while deeply comforting, is not as enduring as it may seem. Its foundations, often built on shared values, trust, and identity, can be surprisingly fragile. The bonds that hold a group together are susceptible to strain, and when those bonds break, the fallout can be profound. The fragility of belonging reveals itself in moments of conflict, change, or betrayal, exposing the delicate balance between unity and individuality that defines every community.

In ancient tribes, belonging was reinforced through shared rituals, common goals, and mutual dependence. Yet, even in these tightly knit groups, the cracks could show. A single act of disloyalty, a challenge to authority, or a disagreement over resources could destabilize the entire structure. These moments of tension often forced tribes to confront the limits of their unity, testing whether their bonds were strong enough to weather the storm or if they would fracture under the pressure.

This fragility is not unique to the past. Modern relationships and communities are equally vulnerable. Families are strained by disagreements, workplaces divided by conflicting priorities, and nations polarized by ideology. The ties that bind people together can fray when values shift, when trust is broken, or when external pressures grow too great. The desire to belong, while powerful, is not always enough to overcome these challenges.

One of the greatest threats to belonging is change. As individuals grow and evolve, their priorities and identities may shift, sometimes putting them at odds with the groups they once called home. A person who questions the norms of their community or seeks a different path may find themselves on the outskirts, their belonging revoked. These moments of disconnection are painful, not only for those excluded but also for the group, which must reconcile the loss of one of its own.

Betrayal is another force that tests the fragility of belonging. When trust is broken—whether by an individual or the group itself—the resulting wounds can be difficult to heal. The betrayed may feel isolated, their sense of security and identity shaken. The group, too, may suffer, as the act of betrayal calls into question the very values and bonds that define it. These moments expose the vulnerability inherent in belonging, showing how quickly unity can give way to division.

The fragility of belonging is a reminder that tribalism, while powerful, is not infallible. It highlights the need for intentionality in building and maintaining connections, emphasizing the importance of trust, empathy, and adaptability. Belonging is not a static state but a dynamic process, one that requires constant effort and care. By understanding its fragility, humanity can strive to create bonds that are not only strong but also resilient, capable of withstanding the challenges of change and conflict. This understanding offers a path forward, one that honors the power of belonging while acknowledging its inherent complexities.

The Enduring Pull of Group Identity

Group identity, born in the shared experiences of ancient tribes, remains a cornerstone of human existence. It shapes how people see themselves and others, providing a sense of purpose, connection, and belonging. The pull of group identity is a force both subtle and profound, influencing behaviors, choices, and perceptions in ways that often go unnoticed. While it can create bonds that unite and uplift, it also has the power to exclude and divide, reinforcing the complex dynamics of tribalism in modern life.

At its core, group identity is about understanding who we are in relation to others. In the earliest days of humanity, this identity was deeply tied to survival. Tribes developed unique customs, symbols, and stories that distinguished them from their neighbors, reinforcing a collective sense of self. These markers of identity served practical purposes, helping tribes to maintain cohesion and loyalty. They also fulfilled an emotional need, providing individuals with a clear place within the group's hierarchy and narrative.

As societies evolved, so did the nature of group identity. It expanded beyond familial or tribal ties to encompass larger affiliations, such as nations, religions, and ideologies. Yet, the underlying instinct remained the same: to align oneself with a group that offered meaning and belonging. This alignment shaped not only personal identity but also how individuals related to the world around them. To be part of a group was to share in its triumphs and defeats, its values and goals, its vision of the future.

The pull of group identity is particularly strong because it speaks to the human desire for significance. To belong to a group is to matter, to be part of something larger than oneself. This connection can inspire acts of extraordinary courage and selflessness, as individuals place the needs of the group above their own. It can also provide a sense of stability in uncertain times, grounding individuals in a collective identity that feels enduring and secure.

Yet, the pull of group identity is not without its challenges. The same forces that bind people together can also push others away. When group identity becomes rigid or exclusionary, it creates barriers that hinder understanding and cooperation. Loyalty to the group can breed suspicion of outsiders, reinforcing stereotypes and perpetuating divisions. This dynamic is evident in everything from political polarization to interfaith conflicts, where the desire to protect one's group often comes at the expense of unity and empathy.

Group identity also shapes how individuals perceive themselves. It can be a source of pride and confidence, but it can also create pressure to conform, suppressing individuality and dissent. The fear of being ostracized often leads people to align their behaviors and beliefs with the group, even when it conflicts with their personal values. This tension between self-expression and group loyalty is a hallmark of tribalism, revealing the complexity of human relationships and the challenges of balancing unity with diversity.

The enduring pull of group identity is a testament to its power and significance. It has the ability to connect and inspire, to provide meaning and purpose. Yet, it also demands vigilance, as its potential to divide is as great as its capacity to unite. By understanding the dynamics of group identity, humanity can navigate its influence with greater awareness, fostering connections that celebrate shared values while respecting individual differences. In doing so, the bonds of belonging can become not just stronger but also more inclusive, reflecting the best of what tribalism has to offer.

The Complexity of Modern Tribes

In today's world, the instinct to form tribes remains as strong as ever, though its manifestations have taken on new and intricate forms. Modern tribes are no longer defined by shared geography or direct survival needs but by ideologies, interests, professions, and even virtual connections. The evolution of these tribes reflects the profound adaptability of the human drive to belong, yet it also reveals the complexity of maintaining unity in an increasingly fragmented world.

Digital communities are among the most striking examples of modern tribes. Online platforms have created spaces where people from vastly different backgrounds can connect over shared interests, values, or goals. From fan groups and gaming communities to political movements and advocacy networks, these digital tribes offer a sense of belonging that transcends physical boundaries. Yet, the same tools that foster connection often amplify division. Algorithms that curate content to align with a group's preferences reinforce echo chambers, where opposing viewpoints are minimized or vilified. In this virtual landscape, tribal loyalty can deepen, but so can the polarization between groups.

In professional and social spheres, tribalism takes on a subtler yet equally powerful form. Workplaces often operate with tribal dynamics, where loyalty to a team or organization shapes decisions and interactions. Social groups, whether based on hobbies, lifestyles, or cultural affiliations, create bonds that provide identity and support. While these tribes can be enriching, offering opportunities for growth and collaboration, they can also become exclusive, limiting engagement with those outside the group.

Modern tribes also thrive in the realm of ideology. Political affiliations, religious movements, and social causes inspire fierce loyalty among their adherents. These tribes rally around shared beliefs and values, creating a collective identity that offers purpose and direction. However, ideological tribes are particularly prone to conflict, as their members often view those with differing perspectives as threats. The resulting polarization not only divides societies but also stifles dialogue, reducing complex issues to binary choices.

The complexity of modern tribes lies in their dual nature. On one hand, they fulfill the timeless human need for connection, providing support, identity, and a sense of purpose. On the other hand, they perpetuate the divisions that have always accompanied tribalism, creating barriers that hinder understanding and cooperation. The challenge of navigating these dynamics is greater than ever, as the interconnectedness of the modern world brings tribes into constant and often contentious contact.

Understanding modern tribes requires recognizing both their potential and their pitfalls. They are a testament to humanity's enduring drive to belong, but they also reflect the ongoing tension between unity and division. By examining the ways in which tribalism adapts to contemporary life, we gain insight into the forces that shape our relationships and societies, offering a foundation for addressing the challenges of polarization and exclusion. In the complexity of modern tribes lies the key to understanding how humanity can balance the need for belonging with the pursuit of a more inclusive and harmonious world.

A Reflection on Belonging

The instinct to belong is as ancient as humanity itself, a force that has guided individuals and shaped societies throughout history. It is a thread that weaves through the earliest tribes, where survival depended on unity, to the modern communities, workplaces, and virtual spaces that define contemporary life. This drive is both a gift and a challenge, offering the warmth of connection while often creating the barriers of exclusion. In its complexity, belonging reveals the best and the worst of what it means to be human.

The stories of loyalty and betrayal, inclusion and exclusion, illustrate the dual nature of this drive. Belonging brings comfort and purpose, fostering trust and collaboration, yet it also demands conformity and loyalty that can blind or constrain. The boundaries drawn by tribalism are as much about who is kept out as who is brought in, leaving individuals and societies to navigate the tension between unity and division.

In modern times, the forms of belonging have multiplied, but the underlying dynamics remain the same. The tribes of today—whether digital, ideological, or professional—echo the patterns of their ancient predecessors. They unite and uplift, but they also isolate and polarize. The psychology of belonging, with its deep roots in human evolution, continues to shape how people see themselves and their place in the world, influencing decisions, relationships, and even global conflicts.

To reflect on belonging is to confront its fragility and its resilience. It requires an acknowledgment of the ways it can heal and the ways it can harm. In understanding the complexities of belonging, humanity has the opportunity to move beyond the limitations of tribalism, embracing connections that are not bound by exclusion but enriched by empathy and understanding. The path forward lies not in abandoning the instinct to belong but in expanding its boundaries, creating spaces where inclusion is not a privilege but a shared promise.

As the exploration of tribalism continues, the lessons of belonging offer a foundation for addressing its broader implications. They remind us that while tribalism may be an ancient instinct, its future depends on how we choose to shape it. By examining what it means to belong, we open the door to a deeper understanding of ourselves and the potential for a world where connection transcends division, reflecting the best of what humanity can achieve.

Tribalism in the Digital Age

In the flickering glow of our screens, a new form of tribalism has emerged. The digital age, with its promise of connection and accessibility, has also given rise to divisions that mirror the patterns of ancient tribes. Social media platforms, online forums, and virtual communities have become the gathering places of modern tribes, where people find belonging, express identity, and rally around shared causes. Yet, these same spaces often amplify exclusion, polarization, and conflict, creating echo chambers that deepen the very divides they were meant to bridge.

The algorithms that drive these platforms are not neutral. They are designed to prioritize engagement, feeding users content that aligns with their interests, beliefs, and behaviors. While this can create a sense of belonging within digital tribes, it also fosters echo chambers where opposing perspectives are rarely seen, let alone understood. These curated environments reinforce group identity, validating beliefs and strengthening loyalty, but they also distort reality, making the "other" seem more distant and less human.

In these digital tribes, loyalty often becomes performative. Likes, shares, and comments act as the currency of approval, signaling allegiance to the group. The need for affirmation drives individuals to align publicly with the tribe's values, even when those values may conflict with their private doubts or broader truths. This dynamic creates a pressure to conform, where dissent is not merely discouraged but punished. The fear of being "canceled" or ostracized mirrors the ancient fear of exile, albeit in a virtual form.

The rise of digital tribalism has profound implications for real-world relationships. Friendships are tested, families divided, and communities fractured as online identities spill over into offline interactions. The polarization seen on social media reflects and exacerbates societal divides, turning nuanced debates into binary battles. The tribal instinct, so deeply rooted in survival, becomes a tool for exclusion rather than connection, a barrier to dialogue and understanding.

Yet, the digital age also holds potential for transcending these divides. The same technology that fosters echo chambers can, if used intentionally, create spaces for meaningful dialogue and collaboration. Online communities have the power to unite people across geographic, cultural, and ideological boundaries, offering opportunities for empathy and learning that were once unimaginable. The challenge lies in navigating these spaces with awareness, resisting the pull of tribalism while embracing the possibilities for connection.

As humanity grapples with the complexities of the digital age, the lessons of tribalism remain as relevant as ever. The instinct to belong, to find identity within a group, is not inherently harmful, but it requires careful stewardship in a world where the boundaries of tribe are no longer physical but virtual. By understanding the dynamics of digital tribalism, society can begin to chart a path forward—one that honors the need for belonging while striving for a broader, more inclusive understanding of what it means to connect. The future of tribalism, in many ways, will be written in the light of our screens.

The digital age, for all its complexity, seems to echo the world before the Tower of Babel—a time when humanity spoke with one voice and shared a common language. Technology has bridged vast distances, creating a global network where ideas and information flow seamlessly across borders. Yet, like that ancient moment, this convergence carries a duality. The unity fostered by a singular digital "language"—a common medium for connection—has not eliminated division but instead amplified it. Just as the Tower of Babel's builders sought to reach the heavens and found themselves scattered, humanity's technological ascent has revealed both its potential for unity and its capacity for fragmentation. The modern world teeters on the edge of repeating history, its global voice echoing with both promise and peril, calling us to choose how we will build—or rebuild—the foundations of connection.

The world's reversion to a metaphorical Tower of Babel through technology—where one digital "language" connects humanity—comes with significant consequences, both promising and perilous. Here are some possible outcomes:

Increased Global Unity

The emergence of a shared digital "language" through technology offers the potential to unite humanity in ways previously unimaginable. With instant communication and access to a nearly infinite reservoir of information, the digital age has created opportunities to bridge cultural, linguistic, and geographical divides. People from vastly different backgrounds can now collaborate, share ideas, and work together toward common goals on a scale that mirrors the vision of a united humanity.

This unity is particularly evident in the face of global challenges. Climate change, pandemics, poverty, and political instability are problems that transcend borders, requiring collective action. Technology enables rapid dissemination of information, mobilization of resources, and coordinated efforts to address these crises. For example, during the COVID-19 pandemic, digital platforms facilitated real-time sharing of medical research, enabling scientists from around the world to develop vaccines and treatment protocols in record time. Similarly, global movements advocating for human rights, environmental protection, and social justice have used digital tools to amplify their voices, rally support, and hold powerful entities accountable.

The shared digital language also fosters intercultural exchange, breaking down barriers that once isolated communities. Social media, virtual forums, and collaborative platforms allow individuals to experience diverse perspectives, traditions, and ways of life. This exposure cultivates empathy and understanding, challenging stereotypes and promoting dialogue. As people connect across borders, they begin to see themselves as part of a global community, united by shared values and aspirations.

Moreover, the ability to communicate and collaborate instantaneously has democratized access to knowledge and opportunity. Entrepreneurs in developing countries can connect with investors, students in remote areas can access world-class education, and marginalized voices can gain a platform to share their stories. The shared digital space offers a chance to level the playing field, reducing disparities and empowering those who were once excluded from global conversations.

However, achieving this vision of global unity requires intentional effort. The same tools that connect can also divide, and the benefits of a shared digital language are not automatically realized. Societies must actively work to foster inclusivity, promote responsible use of technology, and ensure that the digital world reflects the diversity and richness of human experience. If done thoughtfully, the reversion to a Tower of Babel-like state through technology could become not a source of division, but a beacon of unity, guiding humanity toward a more interconnected and cooperative future.

Homogenization of Cultures

As technology continues to weave the world into a single interconnected network, the shared digital "language" risks eroding the cultural uniqueness that defines human societies. In a world dominated by a handful of platforms, trends, and digital norms, the voices of smaller or marginalized cultures may be drowned out, leaving a more homogenized global culture in their place. While this digital convergence offers unprecedented access to shared knowledge, it also threatens to dilute the rich diversity of traditions, languages, and identities that make humanity vibrant.

One of the clearest examples of cultural homogenization is the spread of dominant languages, particularly English, as the lingua franca of the digital age. While this facilitates global communication, it often comes at the expense of less widely spoken languages. Entire ways of thinking, storytelling, and expressing identity risk being lost as younger generations, eager to engage in the global digital space, abandon their native tongues in favor of more universally understood languages.

The cultural homogenization extends beyond language. Social media and entertainment platforms, powered by algorithms designed to maximize engagement, prioritize popular content that appeals to the widest audience. This often means that local art, music, and traditions struggle to gain visibility in favor of globally recognizable trends. Hollywood films, mainstream music, and viral internet challenges dominate the cultural landscape, overshadowing regional expressions and leaving local creators to adapt to global tastes rather than preserving their unique voices.

Global consumerism also plays a significant role in this process. E-commerce giants and multinational brands, propelled by digital advertising and online marketplaces, promote standardized products and lifestyles that permeate cultures worldwide. Traditional crafts, local cuisines, and indigenous practices face challenges competing with the convenience and ubiquity of globalized alternatives, leading to the gradual erosion of cultural identity.

This homogenization is not without resistance. Cultural preservation movements have leveraged the same technology to document endangered languages, share traditional practices, and amplify the voices of indigenous and marginalized groups. Platforms dedicated to local storytelling and cultural exchange offer a counterbalance, reminding the world of the value in celebrating difference rather than subsuming it. However, these efforts often struggle for visibility in a digital space dominated by a few powerful players.

The homogenization of cultures underscores the double-edged nature of the digital age. While technology brings the world closer together, it also flattens the rich tapestry of human experience, prioritizing convenience and accessibility over authenticity and nuance. As humanity navigates this shift, the challenge will be to harness the unifying power of technology without losing the depth, color, and diversity that define what it means to be human. The preservation of cultural uniqueness in a shared digital landscape will require conscious effort, valuing the voices of the many over the dominance of the few.

Amplified Division

While technology has created a shared digital "language" capable of uniting humanity, it has paradoxically also deepened divisions. The very tools designed to connect people are frequently weaponized to isolate, polarize, and fragment societies. Instead of fostering understanding and collaboration, these tools often amplify existing divides and create new ones, mirroring the age-old tribal instincts that separate "us" from "them."

Algorithms, the invisible architects of online interaction, play a significant role in this phenomenon. Designed to maximize engagement, they often feed users content that aligns with their existing beliefs and preferences. This creates echo chambers where individuals are exposed to only one perspective, reinforcing biases and deepening ideological divides. In these isolated spaces, differing viewpoints are not just ignored—they are actively mistrusted or vilified. The result is a digital landscape where polarization thrives, and compromise or empathy becomes increasingly elusive.

Social media platforms, once heralded as tools for global connection, have become battlegrounds for ideological and cultural conflict. Political debates devolve into shouting matches, misinformation spreads with unprecedented speed, and individuals are increasingly sorted into opposing camps. The anonymity and distance provided by digital communication further fuel this division, as interactions lack the accountability and nuance of face-to-face dialogue.

Amplified division also manifests in the rise of "cancel culture" and the relentless policing of group boundaries. Tribal loyalty in the digital age demands not just agreement but active and visible alignment with a group's values and norms. Those who deviate, even slightly, are often met with swift backlash, their dissent framed as betrayal. This culture of immediate judgment stifles dialogue, discourages critical thinking, and heightens the fear of exclusion.

The global reach of the digital world means these divisions are not contained within specific regions or communities. They spill over into real-world interactions, fueling political polarization, cultural tensions, and even violent conflict. The shared digital "language" that connects the globe thus becomes a double-edged sword, uniting people within tribes while driving deeper wedges between them.

Despite these challenges, the amplification of division is not an inevitable outcome. Technology's capacity to connect can be harnessed to bridge divides if approached with intentionality. Platforms that encourage diverse perspectives, promote respectful dialogue, and prioritize truth over sensationalism can counteract the forces of polarization. Addressing the amplified divisions of the digital age requires a conscious effort to balance the instinctive pull of tribalism with the broader human need for unity and understanding.

The danger of amplified division is a stark reminder of the power and peril of technology. It reveals how a shared digital "language" can both unite and fragment, calling humanity to confront the tribal instincts that persist in this new, interconnected world. The challenge is not just to mitigate division but to use technology as a tool for building bridges, fostering empathy, and creating a global community that truly reflects the richness and diversity of human experience.

Loss of Nuance

In the rush of the digital age, where speed and simplicity dominate communication, nuance often becomes the first casualty. The shared digital "language" that technology enables has a tendency to prioritize brevity over depth, reducing complex ideas to soundbites, memes, and hashtags. While this approach makes information more accessible and engaging, it also strips away the subtleties and context that are essential for understanding.

The rise of social media epitomizes this loss. Platforms designed for rapid interaction favor short, emotionally charged messages over thoughtful, measured discourse. Debates that would traditionally unfold over hours or days are now compressed into a flurry of comments, retweets, and likes. In this environment, the loudest, most provocative voices often drown out the nuanced ones, creating a culture where oversimplification reigns. Complex issues are distilled into binary choices—black and white, right and wrong—leaving little room for the shades of gray where meaningful solutions often reside.

This erosion of nuance has profound consequences for dialogue and decision-making. Without the context that nuance provides, misunderstandings flourish, and disagreements escalate. Political polarization, for example, is exacerbated when individuals are exposed only to caricatures of opposing views, presented without the depth or complexity that might foster empathy or compromise. Similarly, cultural and ideological clashes are intensified by the oversimplification of identities and values, reducing entire groups of people to stereotypes.

The loss of nuance also impacts personal relationships. In digital communication, tone, body language, and other nonverbal cues are absent, making it easy for messages to be misinterpreted. Nuance requires time and attention—qualities often in short supply in a world of instant messaging and constant notifications. As a result, interactions become transactional rather than relational, eroding the depth and authenticity that are hallmarks of true connection.

This trend is particularly concerning in areas like education, journalism, and public discourse, where nuance is essential for fostering understanding and critical thinking. The pressure to generate clicks, likes, and shares often leads to sensationalism, prioritizing headlines that provoke over stories that inform. The result is a culture where attention spans shrink, and the pursuit of truth is overshadowed by the pursuit of virality.

Yet, the loss of nuance is not an irreversible trend. Technology, when used intentionally, can facilitate deeper conversations and richer understanding. Long-form content, podcasts, and virtual forums offer spaces where complex ideas can be explored in depth. Initiatives that promote media literacy and critical thinking equip individuals to navigate the digital landscape with greater discernment, seeking out context and resisting the allure of oversimplified narratives.

The challenge of the digital age is to balance accessibility with depth, speed with thoughtfulness. By reclaiming nuance, humanity can ensure that the shared digital "language" becomes a tool for understanding rather than division. The richness of human experience lies in its complexity, and preserving that complexity in a rapidly evolving world is essential for building a future where connection is not just broad but meaningful.

Surveillance and Control

In the interconnected world of the digital age, the shared digital "language" also opens the door to unprecedented levels of surveillance and control. Every message sent, every click made, and every interaction recorded contributes to a vast repository of data that governments, corporations, and other entities can access. While this data can be used to improve services and foster innovation, it also represents a growing threat to personal freedom and privacy, transforming the digital landscape into a space where the watchers are always present.

Surveillance has long been a tool of power, but the digital age has elevated it to new heights. Governments can monitor their citizens with astonishing precision, tracking their movements, communications, and even their thoughts through algorithms designed to analyze behavior. In authoritarian regimes, this surveillance is often used to suppress dissent, target opposition, and enforce compliance with state ideologies. Even in democratic societies, the line between security and intrusion becomes increasingly blurred, as measures intended to protect can easily encroach on individual liberties.

Corporations, too, wield the power of surveillance, often in ways that are less visible but no less impactful. The data collected from smartphones, social media platforms, and online shopping habits is used to construct detailed profiles of individuals, predicting preferences and influencing choices. Personalized advertising, while seemingly harmless, is only the surface of this influence. The ability to shape opinions, behaviors, and even elections through targeted content raises profound ethical questions about autonomy and manipulation.

The consolidation of control in the digital age is not limited to monitoring; it extends to shaping the very environment in which people interact. Algorithms determine what information is seen, what voices are amplified, and what is obscured. This control over the flow of information can reinforce existing power structures, silencing marginalized groups and limiting the diversity of perspectives available to the public. The result is a digital landscape that reflects not the fullness of human experience but the priorities of those who control the platforms.

The implications of this surveillance and control reach far beyond individual privacy. They affect how societies function, how trust is built, and how power is distributed. A world where every action is watched and every choice influenced risks stifling creativity, dissent, and individuality—the very qualities that drive progress and innovation. The fear of being monitored can lead to self-censorship, as individuals conform to perceived norms rather than expressing their true selves.

Despite these dangers, the same technologies that enable surveillance also offer tools for resistance and accountability. Encryption, decentralized networks, and platforms dedicated to privacy provide ways to navigate the digital world without surrendering autonomy. Grassroots movements and investigative journalism use technology to expose abuses of power, shining a light on the darker corners of surveillance and control. These efforts demonstrate that while the risks are significant, they are not insurmountable.

The digital age has brought humanity closer together, but it has also made the structures of power more opaque and pervasive. The challenge is to ensure that the shared digital "language" serves the interests of freedom and equality, rather than becoming a tool for domination. By confronting the realities of surveillance and control, society can strive to create a future where technology enhances, rather than diminishes, the human spirit.

Concentration of Power

The shared digital "language" of the modern world has created unprecedented opportunities for connection and innovation, but it has also concentrated power in the hands of a few. A small number of corporations and governments now control the platforms, infrastructure, and data that underpin much of global communication. This centralization, while efficient, raises significant concerns about inequality, accountability, and the balance of power in the digital age.

Technology giants, often referred to as "Big Tech," wield influence that rivals or even surpasses that of nations. Companies like Google, Apple, Meta, and Amazon dominate markets, dictate access to information, and shape the rules of digital interaction. Their algorithms determine what billions of people see and how they engage with the world, subtly influencing behaviors and decisions in ways that are often invisible to the user. This level of control grants these corporations immense economic and cultural power, allowing them to prioritize their interests over those of the public.

Governments, too, have leveraged technology to consolidate power. While some use digital tools to foster transparency and improve governance, others exploit these tools to monitor dissent, control narratives, and suppress opposition. In many cases, governments and corporations work together, with private firms providing surveillance technologies or data analytics services to state actors. This collaboration further blurs the line between public and private power, making it difficult to hold either accountable.

The concentration of power in the digital age also exacerbates existing inequalities. Wealth, resources, and access to technology are disproportionately concentrated in developed nations and urban centers, leaving rural areas and developing countries at a disadvantage. This digital divide creates a world where the benefits of the shared digital "language" are unequally distributed, perpetuating cycles of poverty and marginalization.

Moreover, this centralization creates vulnerabilities. A single company's decision—whether to change an algorithm, censor content, or prioritize certain services—can have global repercussions. The reliance on a handful of platforms means that outages, breaches, or policy changes can disrupt lives and economies on an unprecedented scale. The centralization of data also makes these entities prime targets for cyberattacks, with potentially catastrophic consequences.

Despite these challenges, there are emerging efforts to counteract the concentration of power. Decentralized technologies, such as blockchain, offer alternatives to traditional power structures, enabling greater transparency and distributing control among users. Grassroots movements advocate for stronger regulations, antitrust actions, and ethical practices to hold corporations accountable. Open-source platforms and community-driven initiatives provide spaces where individuals can reclaim agency in the digital world.

The concentration of power in the digital age is both a reflection of humanity's interconnectedness and a warning about the risks of unchecked authority. It underscores the need for vigilance, innovation, and collaboration to ensure that the benefits of technology are shared equitably and its power wielded responsibly. The future of the shared digital "language" depends on creating a balance where connection and progress are not achieved at the cost of freedom and fairness.

Accelerated Spread of Misinformation

The shared digital "language" of the modern age, while enabling instant global communication, has also become a powerful conduit for misinformation. The very features that make digital platforms effective at connecting people—speed, accessibility, and widespread reach—also make them fertile ground for the rapid spread of false or misleading information. This dynamic poses significant challenges for societies, undermining trust, polarizing communities, and destabilizing institutions.

The architecture of social media and digital platforms amplifies misinformation in ways that are both intentional and unintentional. Algorithms designed to prioritize engagement often favor sensational or emotionally charged content, regardless of its accuracy. False information, which tends to be more surprising and provocative than verified facts, spreads faster and reaches more people. A fabricated story or misleading headline can go viral within minutes, shaping public opinion before the truth has a chance to emerge.

Misinformation thrives in the echo chambers created by digital tribalism. When people are exposed primarily to information that aligns with their existing beliefs, they are more likely to accept and share content without critically evaluating its accuracy. This reinforcement of biases deepens divisions, as groups become more entrenched in their views and less willing to engage with opposing perspectives. The result is a fragmented information ecosystem where trust in traditional sources of knowledge—such as journalism, science, and government—is eroded.

The consequences of misinformation extend far beyond individual misunderstandings. It can influence elections, fuel conspiracy theories, and exacerbate public health crises. During the COVID-19 pandemic, for example, the spread of false claims about vaccine efficacy, treatments, and the virus itself hindered efforts to control the disease and protect lives. Similarly, misinformation has been weaponized by the mainstream media to incite violence, manipulate markets, and destabilize political systems, revealing its potential as a tool for those seeking to exploit societal vulnerabilities.

The accelerated spread of misinformation also highlights the challenges of distinguishing truth from falsehood in the digital age. Deepfakes, manipulated videos, and AI-generated content blur the lines between reality and fabrication, making it increasingly difficult for individuals to discern credible information. The sheer volume of content further complicates this task, overwhelming users with conflicting narratives and creating an environment of uncertainty and doubt.

Efforts to combat misinformation have taken various forms, from fact-checking initiatives and content moderation to public awareness campaigns and digital literacy programs. Technology companies have introduced measures to flag or remove false content, though these actions often spark debates about free speech and censorship. Governments and organizations advocate for greater transparency and accountability in the digital realm, aiming to strike a balance between protecting truth and preserving freedom of expression.

The fight against misinformation is an ongoing challenge, one that requires collective action and vigilance. While the shared digital "language" has the potential to connect and inform, its misuse as a vehicle for falsehood underscores the need for responsible communication and critical thinking. By addressing the roots of misinformation and fostering a culture of truth and accountability, societies can harness the power of the digital age to build trust and resilience rather than division and distrust.

Rapid Innovation

The shared digital "language" of the modern world has unleashed a torrent of innovation, accelerating progress at a pace unprecedented in human history. Technology has become a bridge between minds, enabling ideas to flow seamlessly across borders and disciplines. This interconnectedness fosters collaboration, sparks creativity, and propels humanity toward breakthroughs that once seemed like distant dreams.

The digital age has transformed the way knowledge is created and shared. Scientists from different corners of the globe can collaborate in real time, pooling their expertise to solve complex problems. The development of vaccines during the COVID-19 pandemic offers a striking example: researchers leveraged global networks to decode the virus's genetic sequence, design vaccines, and test their efficacy—all within a fraction of the time such processes once required. This rapid innovation saved countless lives and demonstrated the power of collective intelligence.

Beyond science, the digital revolution has transformed industries and economies. Startups with disruptive ideas can now reach global markets with unprecedented speed, bypassing traditional barriers to entry. Entrepreneurs, inventors, and artists are no longer constrained by geography, finding audiences and collaborators in the digital marketplace. Innovations in renewable energy, artificial intelligence, and biotechnology are reshaping how humans live, work, and interact with the environment, offering solutions to some of the world's most pressing challenges.

Education has also been revolutionized by rapid innovation. Digital tools and platforms provide access to knowledge for millions who previously faced insurmountable barriers to learning. From online courses and virtual classrooms to interactive simulations and AI-powered tutors, technology has democratized education, empowering individuals to acquire skills and pursue careers that were once out of reach.

Yet, this rapid pace of innovation is not without its challenges. The constant churn of new technologies can create societal disruptions, leaving some individuals and industries struggling to adapt. Automation and artificial intelligence, for instance, promise tremendous efficiency but also raise concerns about job displacement and economic inequality. Ethical questions about the use of emerging technologies, such as genetic editing and AI-driven decision-making, demand careful consideration to ensure that innovation benefits humanity as a whole.

Moreover, the speed of innovation sometimes outpaces society's ability to regulate and understand it. New technologies can have unintended consequences, as seen in the rise of social media's influence on mental health, misinformation, and polarization. Balancing the promise of progress with the need for oversight and ethical responsibility is a central challenge in navigating the digital age.

Rapid innovation highlights the dual nature of the shared digital "language." It is both a catalyst for progress and a source of disruption, a tool for solving problems and creating new ones. Harnessing its potential requires not only technological ingenuity but also a commitment to values that prioritize equity, sustainability, and the well-being of all. As humanity continues to innovate, the challenge will be to ensure that the tools created enhance life without compromising the deeper connections and purposes that define it. The digital age offers boundless opportunities, but its greatest promise lies in the wisdom with which it is guided.

Loss of Authentic Relationships

In the digital age, where connections are forged with the tap of a screen, the quality of human relationships faces a profound transformation. The shared digital "language" allows individuals to communicate instantly across great distances, yet it often comes at the expense of depth and authenticity. As virtual interactions replace face-to-face encounters, the nuances of human connection—tone, body language, shared presence—are diminished, leaving relationships more fragile and transactional.

Social media platforms and messaging apps, while offering convenience, often encourage superficial connections. The currency of likes, comments, and emojis can substitute for meaningful conversations, creating an illusion of intimacy that lacks genuine engagement. Friendships are quantified by follower counts rather than emotional depth, and relationships are curated for public display rather than private authenticity. This shift has led to a paradoxical experience: feeling more connected while simultaneously growing lonelier.

The loss of authentic relationships is particularly evident in how people prioritize digital interactions over physical ones. A family dinner may be interrupted by the constant buzz of notifications, each message pulling attention away from the moment. Friends sitting together may find themselves scrolling through their phones, their focus divided between the real and the virtual. These patterns create a disconnect that erodes the bonds of trust and understanding that form the foundation of meaningful relationships.

The digital world also fosters a culture of comparison that strains authenticity. Social media encourages individuals to present an idealized version of their lives, editing out imperfections to create a polished narrative. This curated reality can lead to feelings of inadequacy and disconnection, as people compare their behind-the-scenes struggles to the highlight reels of others. The pressure to maintain a certain image can stifle vulnerability, making it harder to form genuine connections based on shared humanity.

While the loss of authenticity in relationships is a significant challenge, it is not irreversible. Many individuals and communities are beginning to recognize the limitations of digital interactions and are seeking ways to reclaim deeper connections. Initiatives that promote digital mindfulness, such as unplugged gatherings and technology-free spaces, offer opportunities to prioritize presence and engagement. Similarly, platforms that emphasize meaningful dialogue over fleeting interactions provide a counterbalance to the superficiality of social media.

The shared digital "language" has reshaped how people connect, but it need not define the depth of those connections. By being intentional about how technology is used, humanity can preserve the richness of authentic relationships while embracing the benefits of digital communication. The challenge lies in finding balance—using technology to enhance rather than replace the moments of true connection that nourish the soul and define the human experience. In the face of a rapidly changing world, the enduring value of genuine relationships serves as a reminder of what it truly means to belong.

Heightened Dependence on Technology

As the digital age weaves its shared "language" deeper into the fabric of daily life, humanity's dependence on technology grows ever more pronounced. From the moment we wake to the glow of a smartphone screen to the instant we fall asleep beside it, technology mediates our interactions, decisions, and experiences. While this dependence brings undeniable convenience and innovation, it also creates vulnerabilities, raising questions about resilience, autonomy, and the balance of power in an increasingly digital world.

The integration of technology into nearly every aspect of life has transformed how we communicate, work, learn, and socialize. Smartphones, smart homes, and artificial intelligence have become extensions of ourselves, tools we rely on to navigate the complexities of modern living. This interconnectedness offers remarkable benefits—instant access to information, streamlined processes, and enhanced productivity—but it also fosters a growing reliance that leaves individuals and societies exposed to disruption.

One of the most significant risks of this dependence is the potential for systemic failure. Power outages, cyberattacks, or technical glitches can bring entire systems to a standstill, with cascading effects on transportation, healthcare, commerce, and communication. The reliance on cloud-based services and centralized data storage further compounds these risks, as single points of failure can disrupt millions, even billions, of lives. The fragility of these systems underscores the need for robust safeguards and contingency plans to ensure stability in a digital-dependent world.

Another consequence of heightened dependence is the erosion of critical skills and knowledge. Tasks once performed manually are now automated, and information once memorized is now outsourced to search engines and digital assistants. While this shift frees up cognitive resources for creative and strategic thinking, it also raises concerns about the loss of self-reliance and problem-solving abilities. The convenience of technology can make individuals and societies complacent, unprepared to function effectively in the absence of digital tools.

This dependence also affects autonomy, as individuals increasingly entrust decisions to algorithms and artificial intelligence. From recommending what to watch or buy to influencing hiring and legal outcomes, these systems shape choices in subtle but profound ways. While they offer efficiency and personalization, they also raise ethical questions about transparency, bias, and the potential for manipulation. The line between using technology and being used by it becomes increasingly blurred.

Despite these challenges, the growing dependence on technology is not inherently negative. It reflects humanity's remarkable ability to innovate and adapt, leveraging tools to solve problems and improve quality of life. The key lies in managing this dependence with intention and foresight, ensuring that technology serves as an enabler rather than a crutch. Investing in digital literacy, fostering resilience, and maintaining a balance between technological reliance and human agency are essential for navigating this new reality.

Heightened dependence on technology is both a testament to its transformative power and a reminder of its limitations. As humanity moves forward, the challenge will be to embrace the opportunities technology offers while remaining vigilant against its risks. The shared digital "language" has the potential to enhance life in extraordinary ways, but its ultimate impact depends on how it is integrated into the human story—whether as a tool that empowers or a force that diminishes.

Potential for Mass Manipulation

The shared digital "language" of the modern world, while connecting people in unprecedented ways, also provides a powerful platform for manipulation on a massive scale. The same tools that foster community and collaboration can be weaponized to influence thoughts, shape behaviors, and control narratives. This potential for mass manipulation raises profound ethical and societal concerns, as it threatens the very foundations of autonomy, trust, and democracy.

At the heart of this phenomenon lies the data-driven nature of the digital age. Every click, search, and interaction generates data that can be analyzed and used to predict and influence behavior. Advertisers, political campaigns, and even foreign actors leverage this information to craft highly personalized messages designed to sway opinions and decisions. The precision of these tactics, often powered by algorithms and artificial intelligence, makes them both highly effective and deeply insidious. Individuals may believe they are acting freely, unaware of the subtle forces guiding their choices.

Social media platforms, with their vast reach and engaging algorithms, have become central arenas for manipulation. Bots and troll farms amplify divisive content, sowing discord and polarization. Misinformation campaigns spread false narratives, eroding trust in institutions and facts. Even the design of these platforms, which rewards sensationalism and emotional engagement, can manipulate users into prioritizing outrage over reason, creating environments where critical thinking is overshadowed by reactive behavior.

The consequences of mass manipulation extend far beyond individual decisions. It has the power to influence elections, shape public opinion, and destabilize societies. The 2016 U.S. presidential election and the Brexit referendum are notable examples of how targeted misinformation campaigns exploited digital platforms to sway outcomes. In authoritarian regimes, mass manipulation is used to control narratives, suppress dissent, and maintain power, demonstrating how this digital phenomenon can reinforce existing structures of oppression.

The psychological effects of manipulation further deepen its impact. Being subjected to subtle and pervasive influence can create a sense of helplessness or mistrust, as individuals struggle to distinguish authentic information from propaganda. This erosion of trust extends to relationships, communities, and institutions, undermining the social fabric that holds societies together. When people feel manipulated, they may disengage from civic participation, leaving power concentrated in the hands of those who wield these tools most effectively.

Addressing the potential for mass manipulation requires a multi-faceted approach. Governments, technology companies, and civil society must work together to implement safeguards that protect against exploitation while preserving free expression. Transparency in how data is collected and used, regulations to hold platforms accountable, and public education initiatives that promote media literacy are critical steps in this effort. Individuals, too, have a role to play, cultivating awareness and skepticism in their digital interactions to resist manipulation.

The potential for mass manipulation reveals the darker side of the shared digital "language." While it connects and empowers, it also creates vulnerabilities that can be exploited for personal or political gain. As society navigates the complexities of the digital age, the challenge will be to harness the power of this new communication medium responsibly, ensuring that it is a tool for empowerment rather than control. Only by addressing these risks can humanity safeguard the freedoms and trust that underpin a thriving global community.

Opportunity for Global Empathy

The shared digital "language" of the modern era holds the potential to foster an unprecedented level of global empathy. For the first time in history, technology allows individuals to connect with, learn from, and understand people from vastly different cultures, backgrounds, and perspectives. This interconnectedness offers humanity a unique opportunity to bridge divides, challenge prejudices, and build a world grounded in mutual respect and compassion.

Digital platforms provide a window into the lives of others, enabling stories to be shared across borders and barriers. Videos, photographs, and firsthand accounts bring distant experiences into vivid focus, allowing individuals to witness the struggles, triumphs, and humanity of people they may never meet. A refugee sharing their journey, an activist fighting for justice, or a scientist working to address climate change can inspire understanding and action in ways that were once unimaginable.

Social media has also given a voice to marginalized communities, allowing their stories to be heard on a global scale. Movements like #BlackLivesMatter and #MeToo have used digital platforms to draw attention to systemic injustices, galvanizing support and sparking conversations worldwide. These movements demonstrate the power of shared narratives to evoke empathy and mobilize collective action, reminding the world of the universal values that connect us all.

Educational initiatives and cultural exchanges have also flourished in the digital age. Virtual classrooms, language-learning apps, and global forums create spaces where individuals can engage with ideas and traditions beyond their own. These experiences broaden horizons, fostering curiosity and breaking down stereotypes. Exposure to diverse perspectives helps individuals appreciate the richness of human experience, building bridges of understanding that transcend differences.

The opportunity for global empathy is particularly critical in addressing shared challenges. Issues like climate change, pandemics, and poverty require collective action, and empathy serves as the foundation for collaboration. When people understand and care about the impact of these challenges on others, they are more likely to support solutions that benefit the global community. Empathy transforms abstract problems into personal calls to action, motivating individuals and nations to work together for the common good.

However, the potential for global empathy is not guaranteed. The same digital tools that connect can also isolate, creating echo chambers and reinforcing divisions. Misinformation, sensationalism, and polarization can overshadow the stories that evoke understanding, undermining efforts to build connections. To fully realize the potential for empathy, society must be intentional in its use of technology, prioritizing truth, authenticity, and inclusivity in digital communication.

Global empathy is one of the most hopeful possibilities of the shared digital "language." It offers a path toward a more compassionate and united world, where differences are celebrated rather than feared. By embracing the opportunities for connection that technology provides, humanity can move closer to realizing the dream of a global community built on understanding and shared purpose. In a world increasingly defined by its interconnectedness, empathy is not just an ideal but a necessity, lighting the way forward in the digital age.

The Dual Nature of the Digital Tower

The shared digital "language" that now connects humanity is both a remarkable achievement and a profound challenge. Like the ancient Tower of Babel, this new global communication network symbolizes humanity's drive to unite, but it also reveals the fault lines of division that persist beneath the surface. The digital age offers boundless opportunities for connection, innovation, and empathy, yet it also amplifies the risks of manipulation, exclusion, and inequality.

The consequences of this interconnected world are as complex as they are far-reaching. Technology has accelerated the pace of progress, enabling rapid innovation and fostering global empathy, yet it has also homogenized cultures, eroded authentic relationships, and concentrated power in ways that demand accountability. The same tools that bring people together can just as easily deepen divisions, spread misinformation, and create vulnerabilities that threaten the very fabric of society.

Humanity now stands at a crossroads. The digital age holds the potential to bridge gaps that once seemed insurmountable, to create a global community where the richness of human diversity is celebrated rather than diminished. However, realizing this vision requires intentionality, vigilance, and a commitment to using technology in ways that uplift rather than divide.

The shared digital "language" is not inherently good or bad—it is a reflection of how it is wielded. As the world navigates this new Tower of Babel, the challenge lies in ensuring that the foundations are built on trust, inclusion, and a shared sense of purpose. Only then can humanity harness the power of this digital connection to create a future where progress and unity coexist, and where the complexities of the human experience are not lost but enriched.

The story of the digital age is still being written, and its legacy will depend on the choices made by those who shape it. In embracing the opportunities and confronting the challenges, humanity has the chance to turn this digital Tower into a symbol not of division, but of collaboration and hope.

The Erosion of Unity

Humanity's history is a tale of both connection and division, and nowhere is this duality more evident than in the erosion of unity brought about by tribal instincts. What begins as a force for belonging and solidarity within a group often fragments into rivalry, exclusion, and conflict when faced with the broader world. These instincts, rooted in the ancient need to protect and preserve, have transcended their original purpose, shaping the rise and fall of civilizations, the divisions of nations, and the polarization of modern societies.

The story of unity eroded by tribalism stretches back to the earliest human communities. As tribes expanded and encountered others, the instinct to safeguard their own often overshadowed opportunities for collaboration. Conflicts arose over resources, territory, and identity, as each group sought to assert dominance or protect what was theirs. Even as societies evolved into city-states and empires, these tribal divisions persisted, creating fault lines that fractured alliances and fueled wars.

One of the clearest historical examples of this erosion can be seen in the political and religious conflicts of medieval Europe. The unity of Christendom, once a powerful force for cohesion, was gradually undermined by tribal instincts manifesting as nationalistic rivalries and denominational schisms. The Reformation, while a profound spiritual awakening, also revealed the dangers of division as Protestant and Catholic factions clashed, splintering communities and shaking the foundations of a shared identity.

In modern times, tribalism continues to undermine unity on both local and global scales. Within nations, political tribalism pits parties against one another, transforming governance into a battlefield where loyalty to the group often outweighs the common good. Policies and progress stall as each side prioritizes victory over collaboration, leaving societies fragmented and disillusioned. At the global level, tribal instincts manifest in nationalism, where allegiance to one's country blinds leaders and citizens to the interconnected challenges humanity faces, from climate change to global health crises.

The erosion of unity is not limited to politics and nations; it seeps into every aspect of human interaction. In workplaces, rivalries between departments or factions undermine organizational goals. In communities, cultural and ideological divides foster mistrust and isolation. Even in families, tribal instincts can create fractures, as members align themselves with different values or perspectives. The instinct to protect and prioritize one's own often comes at the expense of broader understanding and cooperation.

The consequences of this erosion are profound. Trust, the foundation of unity, is replaced by suspicion. Shared values give way to competing agendas. The sense of a common purpose, which once bound people together, dissolves, leaving societies vulnerable to stagnation, conflict, and decline. The dream of unity, while still present, feels increasingly distant, overshadowed by the forces of division.

Yet, even as tribalism erodes unity, it also offers a lesson. The same instincts that divide can also unite, if channeled toward a broader understanding of belonging. The challenge lies in expanding the boundaries of the tribe, reimagining "us" to include not just those who share our language, culture, or ideology, but all of humanity. This requires a conscious effort to confront the patterns of division, to bridge the gaps between groups, and to foster trust where it has been lost.

The erosion of unity is not an inevitable outcome of tribalism—it is a choice. By understanding the forces that drive division, humanity can begin to counteract them, building a foundation for unity that is not confined by the limits of tribal instincts but enriched by the diversity of the human experience. In confronting the challenges of tribalism, the opportunity to reclaim and redefine unity becomes not only possible but essential for the future of a connected world.

Historical Lessons of Fragmentation

History is a testament to the delicate balance between unity and division. Time and again, civilizations have risen on the strength of shared purpose, only to falter when tribal instincts fractured that cohesion. The lessons of these historical moments offer profound insights into the dangers of division and the enduring challenge of maintaining unity.

The fall of the Roman Empire remains one of the most striking examples of unity eroded by tribalism. At its height, Rome's vast territories were bound together by a shared identity, legal system, and infrastructure. Yet, as internal divisions grew—between rich and poor, urban centers and rural provinces, and various political factions—the bonds that held the empire together weakened. External pressures, such as invasions by Germanic tribes, only exacerbated these divisions. What had once been a powerful, unified entity dissolved into fragmented kingdoms, each prioritizing its survival over the greater whole.

Religious conflicts have also underscored the perils of division. The Thirty Years' War, a devastating conflict in 17th-century Europe, arose from tribal allegiances to different Christian denominations. What began as a dispute over faith quickly spiraled into a brutal struggle for political power, leaving millions dead and entire regions ravaged. The war serves as a stark reminder of how shared spiritual ideals can be overshadowed by the divisive pull of tribalism when loyalty to sectarian identity outweighs a broader commitment to unity.

In the modern era, the partition of India and Pakistan in 1947 highlights the human cost of division. The drawing of borders along religious lines, driven by tribal instincts to protect and separate, led to mass migrations, violence, and the loss of millions of lives. The lingering tensions between the two nations serve as a sobering example of how tribal divisions can cast long shadows, hindering reconciliation and progress for generations.

Even within democracies, tribalism threatens the fabric of unity. The American Civil War revealed the depths of division within a nation that prided itself on shared values of liberty and equality. The sectionalism between North and South, rooted in economic, cultural, and ideological differences, culminated in a conflict that nearly tore the country apart. The scars of that war remain, a reminder of how tribal instincts can undermine the principles of a unified society.

These historical lessons illuminate a recurring pattern: when tribalism supersedes shared identity, unity falters. Whether driven by political, religious, or cultural divisions, the consequences of fragmentation are profound—lost lives, shattered communities, and stalled progress. Yet, they also offer hope, for they reveal the resilience of humanity's desire for unity. Time and again, even in the wake of division, people have sought to rebuild, to bridge the gaps that separate them, and to envision a future where unity is stronger than the forces that threaten it.

The stories of fragmentation serve as both warning and inspiration. They challenge humanity to recognize the costs of division and to prioritize the bonds that hold societies together. In understanding these historical lessons, the path forward becomes clearer: one that values connection over conflict, inclusivity over exclusion, and shared purpose over the allure of tribal loyalty. The past may be marked by division, but the future need not be, provided we heed the lessons of those who came before us.

Modern Manifestations of Division

The tribal instincts that fragmented empires and ignited conflicts in the past now manifest in new and equally insidious ways. In the modern world, division often arises not from physical borders or warring factions, but from ideological divides, cultural tensions, and the hyper-connectivity of the digital age. These contemporary forms of division threaten the cohesion of communities, nations, and even the global order.

Political polarization stands as one of the most visible manifestations of modern tribalism. In democracies around the world, political discourse has devolved into battles of loyalty rather than debates of principle. Parties and their supporters often prioritize winning over governance, treating compromise as betrayal. Media outlets, catering to ideological tribes, amplify this polarization by presenting tailored narratives that reinforce group identity while vilifying opponents. The result is a fractured public sphere, where collaboration becomes rare, and shared goals are overshadowed by partisan conflict.

Cultural divisions, too, have deepened in an era of globalization. While technology and trade have brought diverse cultures into closer contact, they have also heightened awareness of differences, sometimes fostering mistrust and resentment. Debates over immigration, multiculturalism, and national identity often reflect these tensions, as groups struggle to reconcile the preservation of their own traditions with the realities of an interconnected world. The rise of nationalist movements in many countries underscores how tribal instincts can resurface, drawing lines between "native" and "other" in ways that erode unity.

In workplaces and institutions, tribal dynamics often emerge in subtler but no less impactful ways. Teams may become siloed, prioritizing their own objectives over the broader mission of the organization. Rivalries between departments or factions can hinder innovation, as collaboration gives way to competition. These internal divisions, while less dramatic than political or cultural conflicts, reveal the pervasive nature of tribalism and its ability to undermine unity even in structured environments.

The digital age has also introduced new arenas for division. Social media, once heralded as a tool for global connection, has become a battleground for ideological tribes. Algorithms designed to maximize engagement create echo chambers, where individuals are exposed only to information that aligns with their existing beliefs. This isolation fosters hostility toward opposing perspectives, fueling a cycle of misunderstanding and mistrust. The digital world, while expansive, has ironically become a space where divisions are amplified rather than bridged.

The consequences of these modern manifestations of division are profound. They erode trust in institutions, weaken social bonds, and create environments where progress is stalled by infighting. Communities become fragmented, nations lose their sense of common purpose, and global challenges remain unaddressed as groups focus inward rather than outward. The promise of unity, so central to human progress, feels increasingly out of reach in a world where tribal instincts dominate.

Yet, even in the face of these challenges, the potential for unity remains. Understanding the roots of modern division is the first step toward addressing it. By recognizing how tribalism shapes behaviors and decisions, individuals and societies can begin to counteract its effects, fostering dialogue, empathy, and collaboration. The divisions of the modern world are not insurmountable; they are reminders of the ongoing struggle to balance the instinct to belong with the need to connect across differences. In confronting these manifestations of division, humanity has the opportunity to reclaim the unity that tribalism so often threatens to erode.

The Fragility of Shared Values

The unity of any society depends on a foundation of shared values—principles and ideals that transcend individual and group interests to create a collective identity. Yet, in a world increasingly shaped by tribal instincts and modern fragmentation, these shared values are under threat. The fragile bonds that once held societies together—trust, mutual respect, and a commitment to the common good—are eroding, leaving communities vulnerable to division and conflict.

Trust is often the first casualty of tribalism. In the face of growing polarization, trust in institutions, leaders, and even neighbors begins to falter. Political scandals, media bias, and the spread of misinformation exacerbate this decline, as people retreat into their ideological tribes, viewing those outside their group with suspicion. Without trust, the ability to work together for shared goals diminishes, and the social fabric that binds communities begins to fray.

Mutual respect, another cornerstone of unity, also suffers in a fragmented society. Tribalism fosters an "us versus them" mentality, where empathy for those outside the group is replaced by judgment and hostility. In public discourse, civility gives way to personal attacks, and debates become battles for dominance rather than opportunities for understanding. The loss of respect for differing perspectives deepens divides, making it harder to find common ground and build consensus.

The erosion of shared values is perhaps most evident in the decline of the common good as a guiding principle. When loyalty to a tribe takes precedence over broader societal concerns, decisions are made not for the benefit of all but to advance the interests of the few. This dynamic is visible in politics, where partisanship often trumps policy, and in global affairs, where nations prioritize short-term gains over collective action on issues like climate change and human rights. The result is a world where progress stalls and challenges go unaddressed, as unity is sacrificed on the altar of tribal loyalty.

The fragility of shared values is further compounded by the rise of relativism, where the absence of universal standards allows tribes to justify their actions based solely on internal logic. Without a commitment to overarching principles of justice, fairness, and humanity, societies risk descending into moral fragmentation, where each group defines right and wrong according to its own interests. This lack of common ethical grounding fuels conflict and undermines efforts to create cohesive, inclusive communities.

Despite these challenges, the erosion of shared values is not irreversible. Societies can rebuild trust, respect, and a commitment to the common good by fostering dialogue, promoting education, and emphasizing the importance of empathy and understanding. Efforts to address systemic inequalities, combat misinformation, and encourage civic engagement can also strengthen the bonds that hold communities together. By focusing on what unites rather than divides, humanity can begin to restore the shared values that are essential for unity.

The fragility of shared values serves as both a warning and a call to action. It highlights the consequences of unchecked tribalism while underscoring the importance of intentional efforts to preserve and strengthen the principles that bind us. In confronting the forces that threaten unity, there lies an opportunity to create a more resilient and inclusive society, one where shared values are not a relic of the past but a foundation for the future.

A Path Toward Reconciliation

Even in the face of deep divisions and the erosion of unity, the possibility of reconciliation remains. History is replete with moments where fractured communities have come together, rebuilding trust and forging new bonds of understanding. These stories of healing and cooperation remind us that while tribalism can divide, it does not have to define the human experience. The path toward reconciliation begins with a commitment to bridge the divides that tribal instincts create, fostering dialogue, empathy, and a renewed sense of shared purpose.

Reconciliation requires a willingness to confront the root causes of division. This means acknowledging the ways in which tribalism has shaped perceptions, behaviors, and policies, often at the expense of inclusivity and understanding. It involves listening to voices that have been marginalized, addressing historical grievances, and creating spaces where diverse perspectives can be shared without fear of judgment or exclusion. The process is neither quick nor easy, but it is essential for building trust and mutual respect.

Dialogue lies at the heart of reconciliation. True dialogue goes beyond mere debate or negotiation—it is a process of seeking understanding, where participants approach one another with humility and a genuine desire to learn. In communities divided by ideology, culture, or experience, dialogue can reveal common values and shared concerns, highlighting the humanity that exists on both sides of a divide. By fostering open and respectful communication, societies can begin to dismantle the barriers that tribalism erects.

Empathy is another cornerstone of reconciliation. The ability to see the world through another's eyes, to feel their joys and struggles, is a powerful antidote to the "us versus them" mentality. Empathy challenges stereotypes, softens prejudices, and builds the emotional connections necessary for unity. It transforms the abstract "other" into a neighbor, a colleague, a friend—someone whose well-being is intrinsically linked to one's own.

Practical actions also play a critical role in reconciliation. Initiatives that promote collaboration across divides—whether through community projects, cultural exchanges, or shared goals—create opportunities for connection and cooperation. Educational programs that emphasize critical thinking, media literacy, and the importance of shared values can counteract the effects of polarization and misinformation. Policy changes that address systemic inequalities and ensure representation for all groups signal a commitment to fairness and inclusion.

The path toward reconciliation is not without obstacles. It requires patience, courage, and a willingness to embrace vulnerability. It demands that individuals and groups set aside their grievances, not to forget the past, but to envision a future where unity takes precedence over division. It calls for leaders who are not only skilled but principled, capable of inspiring trust and guiding their communities toward healing.

Reconciliation is both a challenge and an opportunity. It asks humanity to confront the limitations of tribal instincts while embracing the potential for connection and collaboration. It is a reminder that unity is not the absence of difference but the ability to move forward together despite those differences. As societies grapple with the divisions of the modern world, the path toward reconciliation offers a way to reclaim the promise of unity, creating a future where the bonds of belonging are stronger than the forces that seek to tear them apart.

Reflection on The Erosion of Unity

The story of unity and its erosion is one of humanity's oldest and most enduring narratives. It is the tale of tribes that grew into nations, of shared values that faltered under the weight of division, and of communities torn apart by the very instincts that once brought them together. From ancient empires to modern democracies, the fragile balance between belonging and exclusion has shaped the course of human history, leaving a legacy of both progress and fragmentation.

The forces that erode unity—tribalism, polarization, and mistrust—are deeply rooted in human nature, yet they are not insurmountable. The same instincts that divide can also be harnessed to build bridges and foster connection. Unity does not require uniformity, nor does it demand the erasure of differences. Instead, it calls for a shared commitment to understanding, respect, and a collective vision for the future.

The erosion of unity reminds us of the cost of division, but it also offers hope. It shows that unity, though fragile, is resilient. It can be rebuilt through dialogue, empathy, and collaboration. It can be strengthened by confronting the forces that threaten it and embracing the diversity that enriches it. The challenge of unity is not to eliminate difference but to navigate it with grace and intention, recognizing that the threads of connection are what hold the human story together.

As the modern world grapples with the complexities of tribalism, the lessons of history and the promise of reconciliation provide a path forward. They invite us to imagine a world where unity is not just an aspiration but a reality—a world where the ties that bind us are stronger than the forces that seek to divide. In reflecting on the erosion of unity, we are reminded that the work of connection is ongoing, a testament to the enduring potential of humanity to rise above its divisions and move toward a shared purpose.

A Moral Perspective on Tribes and Division

In the quiet struggle of human conscience, tribal loyalty whispers its seductive promise: safety, belonging, and purpose. To stand with one's tribe is often seen as the ultimate virtue, a demonstration of unwavering faithfulness to one's people. Yet, within this allegiance lies a paradox, for the very loyalty that unites a group can also blind its members to broader truths, fostering exclusion, injustice, and moral compromise. Tribalism, at its heart, challenges the delicate balance between loyalty and morality, between what is best for the group and what is right for the whole.

The moral dilemmas of tribalism are as ancient as humanity itself. In the earliest tribes, the survival of the group depended on collective effort and unity, and loyalty to the tribe was a matter of life and death. Acts of defiance or disobedience were seen not only as personal failings but as existential threats to the entire community. Over time, this instinct evolved into a deeply ingrained ethic, where prioritizing the needs of the tribe above all else became a hallmark of virtue. However, what began as a survival mechanism grew into a force that often prioritized the group's interests over justice, fairness, or compassion.

Even today, the pull of tribal loyalty exerts a powerful influence on moral reasoning. A political party demands unwavering allegiance, even when its policies conflict with personal ethics. A cultural group defends its traditions, despite evidence of harm to those within or outside the group. The instinct to protect and prioritize one's tribe can overshadow the universal principles of empathy and equity, creating a moral blind spot where the ends justify the means.

The consequences of this dynamic are profound. Tribalism fosters an "us versus them" mentality, where the moral worth of an action is judged not by its intrinsic value but by its alignment with the group's goals. Acts of deception, exclusion, or even violence may be justified if they serve the tribe's interests, while virtues like honesty, kindness, and fairness are set aside as liabilities in the face of competition. In this way, tribalism warps moral frameworks, reducing complex ethical questions to simplistic calculations of loyalty.

Nowhere is this tension more evident than in the divisions among church denominations. The Church, called to be a unified body reflecting the love and truth of Christ, has often succumbed to the same tribal instincts that divide secular communities. Denominations, born of theological and cultural differences, have solidified into tribes that prioritize their distinctiveness over their shared mission. The result is a fractured witness, where believers are often more concerned with defending their denominational identity than with embodying the unity and grace they proclaim.

These divisions distract from the Church's central purpose, creating barriers that hinder its ability to engage the world with a unified voice. The message of Christ, which transcends culture and tradition, is too often obscured by internal disputes over doctrine, practice, or hierarchy. The tribalism of denominations reflects not the diversity of the body of Christ but the fragmentation of a world that desperately needs the hope and healing the Church is meant to offer.

Yet, the moral challenges of tribalism also hold the seeds of redemption. The same loyalty that can blind can also inspire, calling individuals to prioritize the needs of others over their own. When tribal instincts are reoriented toward universal truths—justice, mercy, and love—they can become powerful forces for good. The key lies in expanding the boundaries of the tribe, in recognizing that the true moral calling is not to protect our own at all costs but to seek the flourishing of all.

As humanity grapples with the moral implications of tribalism, the question remains: how can loyalty and morality coexist? The answer lies in a renewed commitment to the principles that unite rather than divide, to the truths that transcend the narrow interests of any one group. Only by confronting the ethical tensions of tribalism can we hope to build a world where loyalty is not a barrier to justice but a bridge to understanding.

Tribalism Within the Church

The Church, envisioned as a beacon of unity and a reflection of divine love, has not escaped the grasp of tribalism. Across centuries and continents, the Body of Christ has splintered into countless denominations, each claiming a piece of the truth while drawing lines that separate rather than unite. What began as a shared mission to embody Christ's teachings has, in many instances, devolved into a fragmented assembly of competing factions, each tribe fiercely guarding its doctrinal distinctions and cultural practices.

The roots of these divisions can be traced to genuine theological differences, but they have often been compounded by human pride and the influence of cultural contexts. The Reformation, for example, marked a pivotal moment in Church history, where calls for reform and a return to Scriptural authority gave birth to Protestantism. While it was a movement of profound spiritual significance, it also planted the seeds of denominational tribalism. Over time, these differences hardened into identities, creating walls that not only divided believers but also obscured their shared faith.

Denominational tribalism often manifests in subtle yet damaging ways. Believers may approach others not as brothers and sisters in Christ, but as rivals whose practices or interpretations must be challenged. Churches may prioritize their unique traditions over the universal message of the gospel, emphasizing differences in liturgy, leadership structures, or theological nuances. These distinctions, while meaningful in context, can become stumbling blocks when they overshadow the fundamental unity found in Christ.

The impact of these divisions is profound. A fractured Church struggles to present a cohesive witness to a world that desperately needs hope and redemption. The gospel, a message of reconciliation and love, is often drowned out by internal disputes and denominational competition. The tribalism within the Church distracts from its mission, fostering suspicion and mistrust rather than the unity and grace that should define the Body of Christ.

This fragmentation also weakens the Church's ability to address the broader challenges of the modern world. Issues such as poverty, injustice, and moral decay require a unified voice and concerted action, yet denominational divisions often hinder collaboration. Instead of standing together as a testament to God's transformative power, the Church appears divided, its influence diluted by internal conflicts.

And yet, the vision of a unified Church remains. Scripture calls believers to be "one body" with "one Spirit," united in purpose and love. This unity does not demand uniformity; rather, it celebrates the diversity of gifts and perspectives within the Body of Christ while maintaining a shared commitment to the gospel. Overcoming tribalism within the Church requires humility, a willingness to prioritize the mission of Christ over denominational pride, and a recognition that the bonds of faith transcend the lines we so often draw.

The path toward unity begins with a return to the core of the gospel—a message that transcends cultures, traditions, and tribes. It calls believers to embrace one another not as members of separate factions but as co-laborers in God's kingdom. By focusing on the truths that unite rather than the differences that divide, the Church can reclaim its witness, offering the world a glimpse of the love and reconciliation that it so desperately needs.

The tribalism within the Church is both a challenge and an opportunity. It reveals the human tendency toward division, but it also highlights the power of grace to heal and restore. In confronting this tribalism, the Church has the chance to embody the unity it proclaims, demonstrating to the world that true loyalty lies not in allegiance to a denomination, but in devotion to the One who unites us all.

The Ethical Dilemma of Loyalty

Loyalty is often celebrated as a virtue, a hallmark of integrity and commitment. It binds families, communities, and nations, creating a sense of belonging and purpose. Yet, when loyalty becomes blind allegiance, it can distort moral judgment, allowing unethical behaviors to flourish under the guise of group solidarity. This ethical tension—between loyalty to one's tribe and adherence to universal moral principles—is at the heart of the dilemma tribalism poses.

In the context of tribalism, loyalty frequently demands prioritizing the group above all else. This prioritization may seem noble, even necessary, but it often leads to moral compromises. A political party justifies corruption because it aligns with the group's goals. A cultural tradition perpetuates harmful practices to preserve its identity. In these instances, loyalty becomes a shield that deflects accountability, excusing actions that would otherwise be condemned.

The ethical cost of loyalty is particularly evident in how it fosters exclusion and prejudice. To protect and uplift their own, tribes often draw boundaries that alienate those outside the group. This dynamic can manifest as discrimination, stereotyping, or outright hostility toward "the other." The instinct to protect one's tribe, while rooted in a desire for safety and cohesion, becomes a moral failing when it denies the dignity and rights of others.

This tension is not confined to secular contexts; it is also evident within religious and spiritual communities. Loyalty to a denomination, tradition, or leader can sometimes overshadow loyalty to the teachings of Christ or the broader principles of faith. Believers may find themselves defending actions or doctrines that conflict with the core values of love, justice, and humility. The ethical dilemma lies in discerning when loyalty supports what is right and when it blinds us to what is wrong.

Despite these challenges, loyalty is not inherently at odds with morality. When grounded in universal principles rather than narrow tribal interests, loyalty can become a powerful force for good. It can inspire individuals to stand against injustice, advocate for the marginalized, and prioritize the well-being of others, even at personal cost. The key is ensuring that loyalty does not become an end in itself but remains a means to uphold and advance what is truly ethical and just.

Navigating the ethical dilemma of loyalty requires introspection and courage. It calls for individuals to question their allegiances, to ask whether their loyalty aligns with their values or merely serves their tribe. It demands the humility to admit when the group is wrong and the resolve to act in accordance with conscience, even when it means standing alone.

The tension between loyalty and morality is not easily resolved, but it offers an opportunity for growth. By examining the ethical implications of our loyalties, we can move beyond the confines of tribalism, fostering connections and commitments that reflect the best of what it means to be human. In doing so, loyalty can transcend its limitations, becoming a bridge to unity rather than a barrier to understanding.

The Call to Higher Allegiances

The tension between loyalty and morality ultimately points to a deeper truth: humanity is called to align itself with something greater than tribal interests. While tribalism offers belonging and identity, it often narrows the scope of allegiance to the immediate and the familiar. True morality, however, calls individuals to look beyond these boundaries, to prioritize universal principles over parochial loyalties. This call to higher allegiances challenges the very foundation of tribalism, inviting humanity to embrace a broader and more inclusive vision of connection.

Throughout history, leaders and thinkers have recognized the limitations of tribal allegiance. Philosophers like Socrates and Jesus of Nazareth called for a shift away from exclusive loyalties toward a universal ethic grounded in truth, justice, and love. Socrates, accused of corrupting Athenian youth, refused to prioritize allegiance to the state over the pursuit of wisdom and virtue. Similarly, Jesus challenged the tribalism of His time, calling followers to love not just their neighbors but their enemies, transcending the narrow boundaries of kinship and culture.

This call to higher allegiances is not an abstraction; it is a practical and ethical imperative. When loyalty to the group conflicts with principles of justice or compassion, individuals face a choice: to follow the tribe or to follow their conscience. This choice often demands great courage, as it requires stepping outside the safety of the group to stand for what is right. History is filled with examples of those who answered this call—abolitionists who challenged the norms of their societies, whistleblowers who exposed corruption, and peacemakers who bridged divides between warring factions.

The call to higher allegiances also resonates within the spiritual realm. In religious traditions, faith is often described as a journey of transcending the self and one's immediate affiliations to align with divine truth. For Christians, this means prioritizing loyalty to Christ and His teachings above denominational or cultural identities. It is a call to unity that reflects the prayer of Jesus in the Gospel of John: "That they may all be one" (John 17:21). This unity is not based on conformity but on a shared commitment to love, humility, and service.

In the modern world, the need for higher allegiances is more urgent than ever. Global challenges such as climate change, poverty, and conflict demand collective action that transcends national, cultural, and ideological divides. Tribalism, with its focus on the immediate and the insular, often obstructs these efforts, fostering competition and mistrust. Higher allegiances, grounded in a recognition of shared humanity, offer a path forward—a way to prioritize the common good over tribal interests.

Answering this call requires both individual and collective transformation. It begins with introspection, a willingness to examine one's loyalties and the values they serve. It grows through dialogue and collaboration, as people of different tribes come together to pursue common goals. And it is sustained by a vision of unity that celebrates diversity while rejecting division.

The call to higher allegiances is not a rejection of loyalty but a reimagining of it. It invites humanity to expand its understanding of belonging, to see every person as part of the same human family. In answering this call, individuals and societies can move beyond the confines of tribalism, creating a world where unity is not just a possibility but a reality, rooted in the shared pursuit of what is good, true, and just.

Reflection on Morality and Tribalism

The interplay between morality and tribalism is a profound and often uncomfortable reality of the human condition. Tribal instincts, while rooted in the desire for connection and survival, can lead to moral compromise, exclusion, and division. Yet, within these instincts lies the potential for transformation—a chance to elevate loyalty from a narrow allegiance to a broader, more inclusive ethic.

Tribalism challenges the clarity of moral judgment. It narrows perspectives, drawing lines between "us" and "them" that distort how we view justice, fairness, and compassion. It asks for loyalty, sometimes at the expense of truth, demanding adherence to the group even when such loyalty conflicts with the greater good. This tension reveals the fragility of morality when it is confined within the boundaries of tribal allegiance, yet it also highlights the resilience of the human spirit to seek higher ground.

Throughout history, individuals and communities have demonstrated the courage to confront these challenges, stepping beyond the confines of tribalism to embrace a more universal sense of justice and love. These moments remind us that morality is not static; it is a journey that requires introspection, dialogue, and a willingness to grow. It asks us to recognize the humanity in others, even when they stand outside our tribe, and to prioritize the values that unite rather than the fears that divide.

The divisions within the Church are perhaps the most poignant example of the tension between tribalism and morality. Called to be a light to the world, the Body of Christ has often been dimmed by internal disputes and denominational pride. Yet, the potential for unity remains, grounded in the teachings of Christ and the shared mission to reflect His love. Overcoming this tribalism requires humility, a return to the gospel's core message, and a commitment to seeing one another not as rivals but as co-laborers in the kingdom of God.

In the broader world, the call to higher allegiances offers a way forward. By expanding the boundaries of loyalty to include all of humanity, individuals and societies can begin to address the moral dilemmas of tribalism. This requires intentionality—recognizing the ways tribal instincts shape our decisions and choosing to align those instincts with values that transcend division. It demands a vision of unity that celebrates diversity while fostering collaboration and mutual respect.

The reflection on morality and tribalism is not merely an intellectual exercise; it is a challenge to live differently. It is a call to confront the instincts that divide and to embrace the principles that connect. In doing so, humanity can move closer to a world where loyalty is not a barrier to justice but a bridge to understanding, where tribalism does not erode morality but enriches it through the pursuit of a higher, shared purpose. This journey is not easy, but it is essential, for in reconciling morality with tribalism, we uncover the true potential of what it means to belong— not to a single tribe, but to the whole of humanity.

Tribalism and the Shaping of Identity

The human soul, restless in its quest for meaning, often finds solace in the boundaries of a tribe. Here, amidst the familiar rhythms of shared customs and collective purpose, the raw edges of individuality are softened, and a sense of identity takes root. From the cradle of early childhood to the rituals of adulthood, tribal belonging serves as both mirror and mold, reflecting who we are while shaping who we become. Yet, the identity formed within the bounds of a tribe carries with it both the beauty of connection and the weight of constraint.

Identity, at its core, is a tapestry woven from countless threads of experience, belief, and relationship. For most, these threads are dyed in the colors of their tribe—family, culture, faith, or ideology. A child learns to speak, not in the abstract, but with the cadence and vocabulary of their people. Stories passed down through generations become more than entertainment; they form the framework through which the world is understood. In these early bonds, identity is nurtured, a flame kindled in the hearth of belonging.

As life unfolds, the tribe's role in shaping identity deepens. Adolescents, seeking both independence and acceptance, often find themselves drawn to the pull of a new tribe—peers who offer the promise of belonging outside the family. These moments of transition reveal the dual power of tribalism to connect and to define. To belong is to feel seen, valued, and understood, yet it also demands conformity, a willingness to suppress certain aspects of oneself to align with the group. The individual is both strengthened by the tribe's affirmation and limited by its expectations.

The shaping of identity through tribalism is not a one-way process. The individual, in turn, shapes the tribe, contributing to its culture and character. A single voice can inspire change, challenge norms, or deepen the tribe's shared values. This dynamic interplay between the individual and the group illustrates the complexity of identity formation, where loyalty to the tribe must be balanced with authenticity to self. Yet, the balance is often precarious. When the tribe's demands grow too great, the individual faces a painful choice: to conform and lose a part of themselves, or to break away and risk the isolation of exile.

Modern society complicates this dynamic further. The proliferation of digital tribes offers endless possibilities for connection, yet it also fragments identity into a mosaic of affiliations. A person may find themselves simultaneously belonging to a political movement, a cultural fandom, a professional network, and a religious community, each with its own demands and expectations. The result is a patchwork identity, where the lines between loyalty and self-expression blur, and the question of "Who am I?" becomes increasingly difficult to answer.

The shaping of identity within tribes is a testament to both the power and the peril of belonging. It reveals the human need for connection, the ways in which we are formed by our relationships and the stories we share. Yet, it also exposes the cost of conformity, the tension between the desire to belong and the need to be true to oneself. In this tension lies the essence of what it means to be human: to navigate the complex interplay of individuality and community, to honor the tribe while seeking a higher allegiance to truth and authenticity.

As the chapter of identity unfolds, it becomes clear that the tribes we belong to are not just external—they live within us, shaping our choices, our values, and our understanding of the world. By examining the ways in which tribalism influences identity, we can begin to see not only its power but also its potential to be reimagined. In embracing the best of what tribes offer while transcending their limitations, humanity can forge identities that are both rooted and free, reflections of the unique and universal journey of being human.

The Duality of Belonging

To belong is to experience a profound sense of connection—a thread tying the self to something larger, a place where individuality is embraced within a collective. Yet, belonging carries a shadow, a subtle tug that asks for compromise, conformity, and the quiet submersion of certain truths in service of the group. This duality is the heart of tribalism's influence on identity, a tension that both enriches and complicates the human experience.

In the warmth of belonging, there is security. Within the tribe's boundaries, life gains order, purpose, and meaning. Roles are defined, values shared, and traditions passed down, creating a foundation that steadies the soul. For a child, the tribe offers a framework for understanding the world, a lens through which the unknown becomes navigable. The tribe says, *You are one of us,* and in that declaration, the fear of isolation dissolves.

Yet, this gift of belonging comes with its price. The very boundaries that protect the tribe also constrain it. Belonging, though comforting, can limit the individual's exploration of self, demanding alignment with the tribe's identity even when it conflicts with personal truths. The young artist who dreams beyond the norms of their culture, the scholar who questions long-held beliefs, the believer who wrestles with doubt—all must grapple with the tension between loyalty to the tribe and authenticity to their inner calling.

This duality is not merely a modern phenomenon. Throughout history, it has shaped human progress and conflict alike. The Renaissance, for example, was born from individuals who dared to look beyond the confines of their tribes—artists, scientists, and thinkers who broke free from tradition to explore the unknown. Yet, even in their defiance, they were shaped by the tribes they left behind, their rebellions a response to the identities formed within their cultural frameworks.

In today's interconnected world, the duality of belonging has grown more complex. Technology offers unprecedented opportunities for connection, allowing individuals to join tribes that align with every facet of their identity. Yet, this abundance of choice can deepen the tension, as individuals navigate conflicting loyalties and the pressure to present a unified self in an increasingly fragmented landscape. Belonging, once rooted in physical proximity and shared experiences, has become a fluid and multifaceted negotiation.

The duality of belonging invites a deeper question: Can the self truly flourish within the tribe, or must it always seek something beyond? The answer lies not in rejecting the tribe but in reimagining it. True belonging is not about erasing differences or silencing doubts but about creating spaces where individuality is celebrated within the context of community. It is about expanding the boundaries of the tribe to include not just those who are like us but those who challenge us, enrich us, and remind us of the shared humanity that unites us all.

This tension between the comfort of belonging and the freedom of individuality is a defining aspect of human identity. It calls us to reflect on the tribes we choose, the values we uphold, and the balance we strike between loyalty and authenticity. In embracing this duality, we uncover the richness of what it means to be human—simultaneously connected and distinct, shaped by the tribe yet free to transcend its limits. The journey of belonging is not about finding a perfect tribe but about forging a path where both the individual and the collective thrive, united in their shared pursuit of meaning and purpose.

The Role of Stories in Identity

Every tribe carries with it a treasury of stories, narratives passed down through generations that serve as both a mirror and a map for its members. These stories, whether told around a fire or transmitted through the glowing screens of the modern age, shape how individuals see themselves and their place in the world. They are the myths that define a tribe's values, the legends that celebrate its heroes, and the cautionary tales that warn against transgressing its boundaries. In this way, stories are the architects of identity, building the framework through which both the individual and the group understand their shared existence.

From the earliest days of human history, storytelling has been central to tribal life. In ancient times, these narratives often explained the mysteries of the natural world, offering meaning and order in a chaotic universe. A tale of a great hunt might teach courage and teamwork, while the story of a storm-god's wrath might instill respect for nature's power. These narratives became cultural cornerstones, defining what it meant to belong and setting the parameters for acceptable behavior.

As tribes evolved into nations and civilizations, their stories expanded in scope and complexity. Epic tales like *The Iliad* or *The Mahabharata* not only entertained but reinforced the values and aspirations of the cultures that birthed them. Heroes like Achilles and Arjuna embodied ideals of strength, loyalty, and honor, while their struggles reflected the tensions between personal desire and communal duty. Through these stories, individuals found models for their own lives, patterns of behavior to emulate or avoid, and a sense of connection to something greater than themselves.

In the modern era, the role of storytelling has become even more influential, yet also more fragmented. Digital media allows for an unprecedented proliferation of narratives, each tailored to the preferences of specific tribes. A sports fan consumes tales of triumph and rivalry; a political enthusiast follows the drama of elections and debates. These stories shape not only individual identities but also the identities of the tribes themselves, reinforcing group values and solidifying the boundaries between "us" and "them."

The power of stories lies in their ability to evoke emotion and create meaning. A well-told tale can inspire loyalty, courage, and sacrifice, binding individuals to their tribe in profound ways. Yet, this power also carries a risk. Stories can be weaponized, used to perpetuate division, justify exclusion, or glorify conflict. A narrative that paints another tribe as the enemy can deepen hostility, while a myth that exalts one's own group at the expense of others can blind its members to their shared humanity.

The interplay between stories and identity invites reflection on the narratives we choose to tell and believe. Do our stories build bridges or walls? Do they celebrate diversity or enforce conformity? By examining the stories that define us, we can begin to understand the values and assumptions that underpin our identities. We can also challenge the narratives that limit us, seeking new stories that expand our understanding of ourselves and others.

In the end, the role of stories in identity is both timeless and evolving. They remain the threads that connect us to our past, the anchors that ground us in the present, and the compasses that guide us toward the future. By embracing the power of storytelling with intention and awareness, we can shape identities that are both rooted and open, honoring the tribes we come from while reaching toward a greater unity that encompasses all of humanity.

The Tension Between Individuality and Conformity

The dance between individuality and conformity is one of the most delicate and defining aspects of tribal identity. Every tribe, whether bound by blood, belief, or ideology, offers a sense of belonging that is deeply comforting. Yet, within that belonging lies an implicit expectation: to align oneself with the group's values, customs, and norms. This expectation, while fostering cohesion, often creates tension for the individual, whose personal identity may not always fit neatly within the tribe's boundaries.

To conform is to blend into the collective fabric of the tribe. It is an act of solidarity, a declaration that one is willing to prioritize the group's needs over personal desires. In tribal settings, conformity has often been a matter of survival. The hunter who acted alone endangered not only themselves but also the entire group, disrupting the delicate balance required to thrive in a hostile world. Over time, this instinct for alignment became ingrained, a hallmark of loyalty and reliability.

However, the cost of conformity can be significant. For the individual, it often requires the suppression of unique traits, dreams, or perspectives that fall outside the tribe's accepted norms. The artist in a family of pragmatists, the skeptic in a community of believers, the visionary in a culture of tradition—all face the challenge of reconciling their inner truth with the tribe's expectations. In the act of conforming, the individual may gain acceptance but risk losing a vital part of themselves.

Individuality, by contrast, is the assertion of the self against the tide of the collective. It is the courage to embrace one's unique identity, even when it defies the tribe's norms. Yet, individuality often comes at the price of exclusion. To stand apart is to risk being seen as an outsider, someone who cannot be trusted to uphold the group's unity. This fear of alienation keeps many tethered to conformity, even when it stifles their growth and expression.

The tension between individuality and conformity is particularly evident in moments of societal change. Movements for civil rights, gender equality, and freedom of expression often begin with individuals who dare to challenge the norms of their tribes. These trailblazers, though celebrated in hindsight, often face resistance and ostracism in their time. Their stories highlight the profound cost of individuality but also its transformative power—the ability to expand the tribe's understanding of what is possible and just.

In modern society, the tension between individuality and conformity is further complicated by the proliferation of digital tribes. Online communities offer unprecedented opportunities for self-expression, yet they also enforce their own forms of conformity. A dissenting voice on social media may quickly find itself silenced or excluded, revealing that even in spaces designed for individuality, the pull of the collective remains strong.

This dynamic invites a deeper question: can individuality and conformity coexist within the tribe? The answer lies in the tribe's willingness to embrace diversity as a strength rather than a threat. A tribe that values innovation, creativity, and critical thinking will create space for individuality, recognizing that it enriches the group as a whole. Similarly, an individual who respects the tribe's shared values can find ways to contribute without losing their unique identity.

The tension between individuality and conformity is not a problem to be solved but a balance to be navigated. It reflects the human desire to belong and the equally powerful need to be true to oneself. By acknowledging this tension and approaching it with humility and openness, both individuals and tribes can grow, creating a harmony that honors the collective while celebrating the distinctiveness of each member. This balance is not only the key to thriving communities but also to the fuller expression of what it means to be human.

The Influence of Cognitive Biases

The human mind, while capable of remarkable complexity, is also governed by biases—mental shortcuts that shape how we perceive the world and make decisions. These cognitive biases are neither inherently good nor bad; they exist to help us process vast amounts of information efficiently. Yet, in the context of tribalism and identity, they play a significant role in reinforcing group boundaries and perpetuating division.

Confirmation bias, one of the most pervasive cognitive tendencies, influences how individuals seek, interpret, and remember information. Within a tribe, confirmation bias reinforces group narratives, as members prioritize information that aligns with their beliefs and dismiss evidence that contradicts them. This bias creates a self-reinforcing loop, where group ideology becomes increasingly rigid, and dissenting perspectives are seen as threats rather than opportunities for growth.

The in-group bias adds another layer to tribal identity. People instinctively favor those within their own tribe, attributing positive qualities to members and excusing their shortcomings. Conversely, those outside the tribe are often viewed with suspicion or hostility, their actions interpreted in the worst possible light. This bias fosters solidarity within the group but also deepens divisions, making collaboration and understanding between tribes more difficult.

Another powerful force is the anchoring bias, where individuals rely too heavily on the first piece of information they receive. Within a tribal context, the narratives introduced early in one's life —whether through family, education, or culture—become anchors that shape how subsequent information is processed. A child raised in a tribe with strong political or religious affiliations, for example, may struggle to consider alternative viewpoints objectively, as their understanding is anchored in the tribe's foundational teachings.

Cognitive biases also influence how individuals respond to conflict. The availability heuristic, which prioritizes readily accessible examples over broader evidence, often amplifies tribal fears. A single negative encounter with someone from an opposing tribe, for instance, may overshadow countless positive interactions, reinforcing stereotypes and mistrust. This bias creates a distorted perception of the "other," fueling cycles of division and animosity.

Despite their challenges, cognitive biases are not insurmountable. Awareness of these mental tendencies is the first step toward mitigating their effects. By recognizing how biases shape our perceptions and interactions, we can begin to question the assumptions they create. Education, dialogue, and exposure to diverse perspectives help counteract these biases, fostering a more balanced and empathetic understanding of others.

The influence of cognitive biases reveals the subtle but powerful ways the mind reinforces tribal boundaries. They show how deeply tribalism is woven into the fabric of human thought, shaping not only group dynamics but also individual identity. Yet, they also highlight the potential for growth, as the same mind that is prone to bias is also capable of reflection and change.

In exploring the role of cognitive biases in tribalism, we uncover a deeper truth about identity: it is not static but dynamic, shaped by both internal and external forces. By understanding the biases that influence us, we can navigate the complexities of belonging with greater clarity and intention, creating tribes that are not confined by their boundaries but enriched by their openness to others. This shift requires effort, but it is a necessary step toward transcending the divisions that so often define the human experience.

The Fragility of Self-Perception

Tribalism, with its profound influence on identity, subtly weaves into the very fabric of self-perception. How we see ourselves, our place in the world, and our value is shaped by the tribes we belong to and the roles we assume within them. Yet, this self-perception is not as solid as it might seem; it is fragile, vulnerable to external validation, and often dictated by the shifting sands of group dynamics.

Within a tribe, self-perception is frequently tied to the tribe's affirmation. A member's sense of worth and purpose is reinforced by their contributions to the group and the recognition they receive. The athlete in a sports team, the activist in a political movement, the caretaker in a family—all draw their identity, in part, from how their tribe views and values them. This feedback loop of affirmation fosters belonging but also creates a dependency, where self-perception becomes entangled with external validation.

This fragility becomes most apparent when the tribe's view shifts. A person celebrated for their loyalty may face criticism if they challenge the group's norms or question its direction. The loss of tribal approval can lead to an identity crisis, as the individual grapples with feelings of rejection and doubt. The foundation of their self-perception, once steady, now feels unstable, forcing them to confront the tension between their authentic self and their role within the tribe.

The fragility of self-perception is also evident in how individuals respond to external threats to their tribe. When the tribe is criticized or challenged, members often interpret these attacks as personal affronts, as though their own identity is under siege. This reaction stems from the deep intertwining of self and group, where defending the tribe becomes synonymous with defending oneself. In these moments, individuals may become more entrenched in their loyalty, unwilling to question the group for fear of undermining their own sense of self.

Modern life, with its multiplicity of tribes, adds another layer of complexity. An individual may belong to several tribes simultaneously, each contributing to different aspects of their identity. A person might be part of a professional network, a religious community, a political affiliation, and a cultural fandom, all at once. Navigating these overlapping loyalties requires constant negotiation, as the expectations and values of one tribe may conflict with those of another. This balancing act further highlights the fragility of self-perception, as the individual struggles to reconcile competing influences.

Despite its vulnerabilities, self-perception within tribalism also holds the potential for resilience. When individuals root their sense of self in values and truths that transcend the tribe, they become less reliant on external validation. This shift allows them to engage with their tribes from a place of strength and authenticity, contributing meaningfully without being consumed by the group's demands. It also equips them to challenge their tribes when necessary, advocating for growth and inclusivity rather than conformity.

The fragility of self-perception is a reminder of the delicate balance between individuality and belonging. It calls for reflection on the sources of identity and the ways in which tribes shape our understanding of ourselves. By examining these influences with honesty and intention, individuals can cultivate a self-perception that is both grounded and adaptable, capable of thriving within and beyond the boundaries of any tribe.

This journey toward a more resilient sense of self is not easy, but it is essential for navigating the complexities of modern tribalism. It invites us to see ourselves not merely as reflections of our tribes but as unique individuals, shaped by connection yet defined by something deeper—a truth that transcends the fleeting affirmations and shifting dynamics of any group.

The Path to Reconciliation

Reconciliation is not simply the end of conflict; it is the beginning of healing, understanding, and renewal. It is the process of mending the rifts that divide us, not only between individuals and communities but also within ourselves. This path requires more than just forgiveness—it demands a willingness to transcend old wounds and build new relationships based on empathy, respect, and shared humanity. In this chapter, we will explore the steps necessary to move beyond tribal loyalties, to confront the legacies of division, and to discover a path forward that leads to a more united world. The journey is neither simple nor quick, but it is the only way forward if we are to break free from the cycles of discord that have defined so much of human history.

The Freedom to Transcend Tribalism

The very essence of human freedom lies in the ability to transcend the constraints of tribalism, to rise above the narrow definitions that groups often impose on their members. Tribal loyalty, while offering a sense of identity and belonging, can also confine individuals, narrowing their perspectives and restricting their potential. Yet, the capacity to transcend these boundaries is one of the most powerful forms of self-liberation, offering a way to expand one's sense of self beyond the limits of group allegiance and open the door to deeper understanding and more meaningful connections.

Transcending tribalism does not require the abandonment of one's tribe or the denial of the relationships and values that have shaped one's life. Rather, it involves seeing oneself and others through a broader lens—acknowledging the role of the tribe in shaping identity while refusing to let it define every aspect of one's being. It is a movement from belonging that is defined by allegiance to a specific group to belonging that is defined by a shared humanity. This shift allows for the cultivation of an authentic self that is both rooted in history and open to future possibilities.

At its core, the freedom to transcend tribalism is about choice. It is the ability to see and engage with the world not just through the prism of one's tribe but through the lens of universal values —compassion, justice, and love. These principles transcend any particular cultural or ideological framework, offering a foundation for connection that is not bound by the limitations of group identity. When individuals make the conscious decision to align with these higher values, they are able to navigate the complexities of tribalism without being consumed by it.

This process is often challenging. It requires individuals to confront the tribal instincts that have been embedded in their psyche and, in many cases, their very survival mechanisms. To move beyond tribalism means to question long-held beliefs, to embrace discomfort, and to stand in opposition to the forces that seek to divide. The fear of rejection, the loss of belonging, and the weight of isolation are powerful deterrents to transcending tribal loyalty. Yet, this is precisely the point where true freedom begins—when the individual finds the courage to break free from the tyranny of groupthink and embrace a more expansive and inclusive vision of connection.

The freedom to transcend tribalism is also deeply relational. It calls for empathy, the ability to see the humanity in others who may belong to different tribes, who may hold conflicting beliefs or values. In transcending tribalism, individuals begin to see the world not in terms of "us" versus "them" but as a complex web of shared experiences, struggles, and aspirations. This vision creates the possibility for deeper, more meaningful connections, grounded not in shared group identity but in a mutual understanding of the common threads that bind all people together.

Moreover, the freedom to transcend tribalism offers a path toward greater societal cohesion. As more individuals choose to embrace unity over division, the collective mindset shifts. Communities, nations, and even the global society begin to value diversity not as a threat but as a strength, a richness that enhances the shared human experience. The idea of belonging expands, creating spaces where individuals are encouraged to contribute their unique gifts while honoring the contributions of others, regardless of their tribal affiliations.

Transcending tribalism is not about rejecting one's roots or erasing the importance of community—it is about expanding the concept of belonging. It is about recognizing that while tribes offer valuable connections and meaning, true freedom lies in the ability to see beyond those boundaries, to recognize that our identity is not defined solely by where we come from or the groups we belong to but by the values we uphold and the relationships we cultivate with all people.

In this light, the freedom to transcend tribalism is not merely an individual pursuit but a collective endeavor, a journey that calls each person to embrace their shared humanity and the possibilities of unity over division. It is a path that requires courage, vision, and the willingness to move beyond the confines of allegiance to something larger, something that embraces all people, all tribes, and all identities. This freedom, when realized, is the gateway to a deeper, more profound connection to the world and to each other.

The Path Toward Unity

The journey toward unity is not a linear path but a winding road, marked by both progress and setbacks, by moments of insight and periods of struggle. It is a path that requires individuals, communities, and even nations to confront the instincts that divide them, to break free from the constraints of tribalism and build a new kind of connection—one that transcends the boundaries of identity and embraces the shared humanity that unites us all. This path is both a challenge and an invitation, a call to see the world not in terms of "us" and "them" but as a complex, interconnected web of people with shared hopes, dreams, and struggles.

Unity, in its truest sense, is not the absence of difference but the acknowledgment that differences are not barriers but bridges. To walk the path toward unity is to recognize that every person, no matter their tribe, carries within them a story worth listening to, a perspective worth understanding. It is a journey that requires empathy—an openness to hear, to understand, and to respect others even when their experiences or beliefs differ from our own. This empathy is the cornerstone of connection, for it is through understanding others that we are able to build the bonds that hold societies together.

Yet, empathy alone is not enough. True unity requires action—the willingness to move beyond understanding and into the realm of shared purpose. This means actively seeking to create spaces where people can come together, collaborate, and work toward common goals. It means fighting for justice, equality, and opportunity for all people, regardless of their background or affiliation. It is through these shared efforts that unity is truly forged, as individuals begin to see that their well-being is intertwined with the well-being of others.

The path toward unity also requires vulnerability—the courage to face the divisions within ourselves and our communities. To transcend tribalism, individuals must be willing to question their own biases and assumptions, to challenge the narratives that have shaped their identities, and to embrace a broader, more inclusive vision of what it means to belong. This is not an easy task, as it requires letting go of the security of certainty and embracing the discomfort of change. Yet, it is only through this vulnerability that true growth occurs, both on a personal and societal level.

In practical terms, the path toward unity involves building institutions, relationships, and systems that prioritize inclusivity over exclusion. It requires creating spaces for dialogue, where differences can be expressed and explored without fear of retribution or marginalization. It means investing in education and awareness, fostering understanding through exposure to diverse perspectives, and encouraging the exchange of ideas. The goal is not to erase difference but to celebrate it, recognizing that the richness of human experience lies in its diversity and that unity can only be achieved when that diversity is embraced.

At its heart, the path toward unity is a spiritual journey, one that calls individuals to align their lives with higher values—love, compassion, justice, and peace. These values transcend tribal loyalty, offering a vision of connection that is rooted not in shared ideology but in shared humanity. The path to unity is one that recognizes the sacredness of each person, regardless of their tribe, and honors the interconnectedness of all life.

As humanity takes steps along this path, it may stumble, it may falter, and it may encounter setbacks. The forces of division are strong, and tribalism remains a deeply embedded instinct. Yet, the journey toward unity is worth the struggle, for it holds the promise of a world where connection, empathy, and shared purpose replace the walls of separation that have divided us for so long. In walking this path, humanity can create a future that is not defined by tribal boundaries but by the common thread of belonging that binds us all.

Finding Our True Tribe

This chapter calls us to seek a higher belonging, one that transcends the limitations of earthly affiliations and tribal identities. Beyond the borders of culture, ideology, and division, there exists a tribe defined not by human distinctions, but by faith in a loving Creator. This ultimate community, rooted in grace and truth, offers a place where all are united under the banner of love and restoration. In this chapter, we will explore the call to embrace our true identity in Christ, to step beyond the constraints of worldly tribes, and to join a movement of reconciliation, compassion, and transformative love that brings healing to a fractured world.

Embracing a Unified Future

The dream of a unified world is both a lofty ideal and a deeply human aspiration—a world where differences are not threats to our existence but expressions of the richness of the human experience. Yet this vision requires more than mere hope; it demands active participation, a collective effort to weave the threads of our fragmented identities into a tapestry of shared purpose and mutual respect. Embracing a unified future calls for individuals, communities, and societies to choose connection over division, to recognize that the strength of our common humanity far outweighs the limitations of tribal loyalty.

This vision of unity is not about erasing differences or denying the uniqueness of each individual or group. It is about recognizing that, despite our varied histories, cultures, and beliefs, there are fundamental values—justice, love, empathy—that bind us all. It is about choosing to see each person not through the lens of their tribe, culture, or ideology, but as a fellow human being with the same capacity for hope, pain, joy, and struggle. In this shift of perception, the barriers that divide us begin to crumble, replaced by a recognition that we are all part of the same interconnected whole.

The path toward this unified future begins within. It starts with the individual—each person making the choice to engage with the world in a way that transcends the narrow confines of their tribe. It is a call to develop a personal commitment to justice, to empathy, to love. By choosing to embody these values in everyday life, individuals can begin to break free from the tribal instincts that separate us. They can find common ground with others, even when differences remain, and create connections that are grounded in respect and understanding.

At the collective level, this process involves reevaluating institutions, policies, and systems that have historically perpetuated division. It requires fostering an environment where collaboration, inclusivity, and dialogue are prioritized over competition and exclusion. Governments, organizations, and communities must actively work to dismantle structures that divide, replacing them with ones that promote equity, opportunity, and mutual support. This is a difficult task, as it requires confronting deep-seated inequalities and systemic injustices. Yet, it is through this work that a unified future can begin to take shape—a world where every individual has the opportunity to flourish, regardless of their background or affiliation.

The future we aspire to is one in which unity is not just an abstract ideal but a living, breathing reality. It is a world where tribalism no longer defines us but where our shared humanity does. It is a future where people from different tribes can come together, not in spite of their differences but because of them, each person contributing their unique perspectives and talents to the greater good. It is a world where the walls between us are replaced with bridges—where empathy, understanding, and collaboration become the norm rather than the exception.

This vision may seem distant, and the journey toward it may be long and fraught with obstacles. Yet, it is a vision worth striving for, for in embracing unity, humanity embraces its highest potential. As individuals, as communities, and as a global society, we have the capacity to create a future that is not defined by tribal division but by the bonds of shared purpose and mutual respect. The work may be challenging, but it is not impossible. With each step we take toward unity, we move closer to a world where every person, regardless of their tribe, feels truly seen, valued, and connected. In the end, this is the promise of the human spirit—to find strength in diversity and unity in our shared humanity.

The Legacy of Unity

In the grand arc of human history, the legacy we leave behind is not just one of accomplishments, technologies, or ideologies, but the legacy of how we came together despite our divisions. The journey toward unity is not merely an individual pursuit but a collective endeavor that will echo through generations, shaping the world we leave to those who come after us. This legacy, rooted in empathy, respect, and shared purpose, offers the promise of a future where the very idea of tribalism is seen not as a source of division but as a stepping stone to deeper, more meaningful connections.

The legacy of unity begins with the choices we make today. In each moment, we are presented with opportunities to break down barriers—whether within our families, communities, or nations. Each decision to engage in respectful dialogue, to reach across perceived lines of division, to acknowledge the humanity in others, adds to the foundation of a united future. By embodying the values of empathy, fairness, and understanding in our daily lives, we begin to weave a tapestry of unity that will stand the test of time.

In a world that often seems fragmented by ideology, culture, and conflict, the legacy of unity challenges us to imagine a future where differences are not seen as threats but as opportunities for growth and collaboration. It asks us to recognize that the strength of our collective humanity lies in its diversity, and that true unity is not the absence of difference, but the willingness to respect and embrace it. This is a legacy that transcends borders, one that builds a world where everyone has a place, where the rich tapestry of human experience is celebrated, and where the bonds of connection run deeper than the divisions that have historically kept us apart.

The impact of this legacy extends beyond the present moment. As we strive for unity in our time, we are paving the way for future generations to build upon the foundation we lay. The children who grow up in a world where empathy and collaboration are valued over tribal loyalty will carry these principles into their own lives, shaping a society that is not defined by the walls that once divided it but by the bridges that have been built in their place. The story of unity will be passed down through the generations, a reminder of the power of collective effort and the enduring strength of the human spirit.

Yet, the legacy of unity is not solely about what we create for the future—it is also about healing the past. Tribalism has caused immeasurable harm throughout history, creating divisions that have led to war, injustice, and suffering. In working toward unity, we are also engaging in a process of reconciliation, acknowledging the wounds of the past and seeking to mend them. By addressing historical wrongs and fostering understanding between groups that have been divided for generations, we begin to heal the fractures that have shaped our collective memory and create a foundation for lasting peace.

In the end, the legacy of unity is not defined by the absence of conflict but by the presence of understanding and cooperation. It is a legacy that teaches us to transcend the limitations of tribalism, to see beyond the lines that divide us, and to embrace the common humanity that binds us all. The journey toward unity may be long, but with each step we take, we add to the legacy that will one day define the world not by its differences but by its shared values, its capacity for empathy, and its commitment to the well-being of all. This is the legacy of unity— the promise of a future where we are not merely members of separate tribes, but a global family united in purpose, vision, and love.

The Eternal Struggle for Unity

In the tapestry of human history, the struggle for unity is woven with both triumph and tragedy, a constant dance between connection and division. Each era, each society, carries with it the echoes of this age-old conflict—the desire to unite for a common purpose, to stand together as one, and the inevitable pull of tribal instincts that seek to protect, separate, and prioritize the group. It is a struggle that has shaped the rise and fall of empires, the formation of nations, and the ongoing efforts of individuals and communities to transcend the forces that divide them.

The eternal nature of this struggle reflects a deeper truth about the human condition. We are creatures of both belonging and independence, driven by a need to connect with others, yet equally compelled by the desire to assert our individuality. This tension is ever-present, as groups and tribes form to give meaning and structure to human life, yet it is within these very groups that division takes root. The forces that bind us together can, in an instant, be twisted into the forces that tear us apart.

The scriptures, both ancient and modern, speak to this struggle in profound ways. The call to unity is woven throughout the pages of sacred texts, from the promise of peace in the Psalms to the prayer of Christ for His followers to be one, just as He and the Father are one. Yet, these calls are not mere hopes; they are challenges, each one recognizing the difficulty of human unity. "Where there is no vision, the people perish," the proverb tells us, and so it is with unity— without a shared vision, a common purpose, we fall into division. The challenge, then, is to align our visions with something higher than our tribal loyalties, something greater than the groups we form.

In a world filled with polarization, the call for unity feels like a whisper in the wind, fragile and faint. Political divides, cultural rifts, and ideological battles rage across the globe, and it can seem that the dream of unity is hopelessly distant. Yet, it is precisely in this struggle that the deepest lessons are learned. Unity, it seems, is not a static condition to be achieved but a continual striving—a journey marked by both setbacks and progress. It is a goal that requires sacrifice, humility, and, above all, a willingness to see the humanity in others, especially in those who seem so different from ourselves.

The eternal struggle for unity calls us to rise above the pull of tribalism and to embrace a higher calling. It asks us to see beyond the boundaries of our affiliations and recognize the common thread of shared humanity. This is not to erase our differences or deny the unique qualities that each tribe brings to the world. Rather, it is to honor those differences in a way that allows for collaboration, understanding, and peace.

This journey toward unity is not an easy one, and it requires more than just hope or good intentions. It demands action—a commitment to building bridges where walls have been erected, to speaking truth where silence has reigned, and to acting with courage when fear seeks to divide. It calls for individuals to take up the mantle of reconciliation, to be willing to stand in the uncomfortable space between opposing forces, and to extend a hand of peace to those who seem unreachable.

The struggle for unity is eternal because it is an integral part of our human journey. From the first tribes of our ancestors to the complex global society of today, humanity has wrestled with how to balance loyalty to the group with the call to transcend its limitations. And though the road may seem long, filled with conflict and uncertainty, the promise of unity remains a beacon on the horizon—an aspiration that drives us forward, even in the darkest of times.

As we stand on this path, we are reminded that unity is not a destination but a process—a continuous act of choosing connection over division, compassion over judgment, understanding over fear. It is in the pursuit of this unity, in the willingness to struggle together for a common cause, that humanity's highest potential is realized. In this eternal struggle, we find not only the essence of who we are but the future we long to create.

The Promise of a Unified Future

The promise of a unified future is not a distant dream or a fleeting ideal, but a call to action rooted in the present. It is a promise that we are capable of more than the division and discord that often define our world; it is a promise that, despite our differences, we can forge a path forward together. This path is not without its difficulties, but it is one paved with the possibility of transformation—where the very forces that once divided us can become the building blocks of a more compassionate, just, and united humanity.

To move toward this unified future, we must first confront the reality of what divides us. We cannot ignore the divisions of history, the injustices that have shaped the boundaries between "us" and "them," or the tribal instincts that continue to influence our decisions. But acknowledging these divisions is not a surrender; it is the first step toward healing. For only by recognizing the wounds of the past can we begin to address them and move toward reconciliation.

A unified future does not mean that all will think the same, speak the same, or live the same. It is not a future of uniformity, but of harmony—a future where differences are not feared but embraced. Just as an orchestra is made up of distinct instruments, each contributing its own unique sound to a greater symphony, so too can a unified world be made up of distinct cultures, ideas, and identities. The beauty lies not in the erasure of these differences but in the way they come together to create something greater than the sum of its parts.

In this vision of unity, compassion becomes the bridge between divides. Compassion allows us to see beyond the surface, beyond the labels and categories that divide us, and into the hearts of those we may once have called "other." It calls us to listen—not just to hear, but to truly listen, to understand the stories and struggles of those who have been marginalized, to extend empathy to those whose experiences differ from our own. Compassion calls us to act—not just in small, individual acts of kindness, but in large, collective movements toward justice, equity, and peace. It is compassion that turns division into collaboration, suspicion into trust, and fear into love.

This vision of a unified future is rooted in the timeless truths that transcend the temporary divisions of our world. It is a vision that calls for individuals and communities to align their actions with values that are greater than tribal loyalty—values like justice, equality, and human dignity. These values, when embraced by people from all walks of life, form the foundation of a world that is not defined by division but by the pursuit of the common good.

But unity does not come easily. It requires sacrifice. It demands that we look beyond our own interests and consider the well-being of others. It asks that we give up the comforts of certainty and ease to face the challenges of change. The journey toward a unified future is a costly one— one that asks us to confront our biases, break down the walls that divide us, and rebuild our world on a foundation of love and understanding.

Yet, even in its cost, the promise of a unified future offers hope. It is a hope that transcends the darkness of division and lights the way forward. It is a hope that recognizes the power of each individual, each community, and each tribe to contribute to the creation of a better world. And it is a hope that, when embraced, can transform the world—one step at a time, one relationship at a time, one act of kindness at a time.

In the promise of this unified future, humanity finds its greatest potential—together, not as tribes divided, but as a single, interconnected family. The dream of unity is not a mere ideal; it is a tangible reality, waiting for those who are willing to take the first steps toward it. In this promise, we find not only hope for the future but a deep, abiding purpose in the present, as we choose to walk the path of unity, hand in hand with one another.

Moving Forward Together

As our journey toward understanding tribalism draws to a close, the call to action begins. In this chapter, we reflect on our personal tendencies toward division and challenge ourselves to actively build unity in our families, communities, and beyond. With love as our guiding principle, we are inspired to move from awareness to action, fostering connections and breaking down barriers. This chapter leaves us with a hopeful vision of a world where division fades, understanding flourishes, and we move forward together, united in our shared humanity.

The Call to Action: Building a Unified World

The call to action for building a unified world is not a vague aspiration, but a tangible, pressing challenge. It is a summons to rise above the divisions that have long defined us, to choose a path that honors both our shared humanity and our differences. The time has come for individuals, communities, and nations to step forward, not merely as passive observers of a fractured world but as active agents of change. The promise of unity can only be realized if we, together, commit to the work of rebuilding, reconciling, and reimagining what it means to be truly united.

Building a unified world requires intentionality. It begins with the simple but powerful act of reaching out across boundaries, of seeing not strangers but neighbors in those who appear different. It is the recognition that every person, no matter their background, carries with them inherent dignity and value. To build unity, we must first see each other as worthy of respect, as part of the same global family, each contributing to the complex yet beautiful mosaic of human life. The question is not whether we will continue to exist within our separate tribes, but whether we will choose to forge something new—a global tribe defined by shared compassion, understanding, and purpose.

The act of uniting the world cannot be the work of a few; it requires the involvement of many. Communities must embrace the diversity that exists within them, fostering environments where collaboration and dialogue replace conflict and division. Education is key in this endeavor, for the more we understand one another, the less we fear one another. Teaching empathy, critical thinking, and global awareness equips individuals to break free from tribal thinking and see the world through a broader, more inclusive lens. In this way, education becomes not just a tool for knowledge, but a catalyst for unity, opening minds and hearts to the potential for collective action.

On a larger scale, political and social leaders must lead by example, advocating for policies that promote equity, justice, and collaboration. Unity, after all, must be reflected not only in personal interactions but in the structures that govern our societies. Leaders must recognize that true progress is not defined by winning battles or preserving power but by advancing the common good, by ensuring that every voice is heard and every person has the opportunity to thrive. It is a call for governance that transcends party lines, that sees the collective well-being as its highest priority, and that works not to maintain division, but to heal it.

The work of unity also requires reflection and reconciliation. We must look to the wounds of the past, to the injustices and the divisions that have scarred our collective history. Only by acknowledging these hurts, by facing them with honesty and humility, can we begin the work of healing. Reconciliation is not a simple act, nor is it quick. It demands deep vulnerability, an openness to the uncomfortable truths that we would rather ignore. Yet, it is in this act of reconciliation—whether on the global scale or between individuals—that true unity is born. It is a process that requires patience, grace, and an unwavering commitment to the belief that all people, regardless of their past, are deserving of healing and wholeness.

Finally, the call to action demands that we see the work of building unity as ongoing, not as a one-time effort but as a continuous commitment to one another. It is easy to become disheartened by setbacks or discouraged by the magnitude of the task before us. Yet, unity is built in small moments—each act of kindness, each conversation that bridges a gap, each decision that favors the collective good over individual gain. Every person who chooses unity, every community that strives for inclusion, every leader who prioritizes justice and peace is contributing to the larger mosaic of a unified world.

The path toward a unified world is not easy, but it is necessary. It requires all of us to do the hard work of seeing beyond our immediate tribe, of extending compassion to those who are different, and of committing to the greater good. The call to action is not just about changing the world— it is about changing ourselves, about recognizing that the choice to build unity begins within each of us. The world will be unified not by one grand gesture but by millions of small, intentional acts that together form a movement of transformation. It is a movement that begins now, and one that calls us all to participate in building a future where division no longer defines us, but unity, rooted in love and understanding, becomes the foundation upon which we stand.

The Final Vision: Unity in Diversity

In the final vision of a unified world, we find a paradox that, once embraced, becomes the key to the future: unity does not demand the erasure of difference but the celebration of it. True unity is not found in sameness, nor is it achieved through conformity, but in the rich tapestry of diversity where every thread—every unique voice, culture, belief, and perspective—adds depth, color, and texture to the whole. This vision of unity is not one of uniformity, but of harmony—a melody composed of many distinct notes, each contributing to a symphony that resonates with the beauty of human existence in all its forms.

The path to this vision is clear: we must learn to value what makes us different, while recognizing the common humanity that binds us together. Our shared experiences of joy, sorrow, love, and struggle remind us that, no matter our backgrounds, we are united in our vulnerability, our capacity for growth, and our search for meaning. This vision asks us not to dilute our individual identities but to reframe them in a way that aligns with the greater good, a recognition that our differences are not barriers but bridges to understanding, collaboration, and mutual respect.

In a world where tribalism has often led to conflict, division, and suffering, the call to unity in diversity offers both a challenge and a promise. It challenges us to move beyond the fear and distrust that have too often defined our interactions with those who are different. It asks us to embrace the discomfort of engaging with the "other," to listen with empathy, to question our assumptions, and to act with compassion. And it promises that, in doing so, we can create a world where division gives way to connection, where the walls between us are replaced with bridges, and where the vast diversity of human experience becomes the wellspring of creativity, innovation, and peace.

This vision is not a distant dream but a present possibility, one that is realized in every action taken to break down the barriers of division and build up the bonds of unity. Each time we choose empathy over judgment, understanding over suspicion, and collaboration over competition, we take one step closer to a world where unity is not just an abstract ideal but a lived reality. Each individual act of kindness, each conversation that bridges ideological gaps, each effort to understand rather than to condemn contributes to the larger vision of a world where humanity is united, not in spite of our differences, but because of them.

The power of this vision lies in its ability to transform. When we learn to see the diversity of human experience not as a threat but as a source of strength, we begin to build a world that reflects the richness of our collective potential. A world where individuals are not confined by their tribal identities but are free to express their unique gifts while contributing to a greater shared purpose. This is a world where unity is not about homogenizing culture, erasing differences, or silencing voices, but about creating space for everyone to belong, to contribute, and to thrive.

In this world, the promise of unity is fulfilled not through the absence of conflict, but through the presence of respect, understanding, and mutual care. It is a world where each tribe, each community, each individual has the freedom to express their identity without fear of rejection, and where the collective strength of humanity is drawn from the diverse voices that speak to the shared values of justice, peace, and love. It is a vision that sees diversity not as an obstacle to unity but as its foundation—built on the understanding that our differences do not divide us, but rather, they enrich us, making the whole stronger, more resilient, and more beautiful.

The final vision of unity in diversity is not only possible, but it is necessary. In a world that is increasingly interconnected, the ability to embrace diversity while striving for unity will determine the future of our global community. It is a vision rooted in hope, grounded in the belief that humanity, in all its complexity and beauty, is capable of transcending the divisions that have too long kept us apart. The work may be difficult, and the road may be long, but with each step toward this vision, we move closer to a world where unity is not a distant dream but a living, breathing reality—one where the full spectrum of human diversity is celebrated as the greatest strength of all.

A New Era of Collective Humanity

As we stand on the threshold of a new era, the possibilities for a collective humanity are more promising than ever. The interconnectedness of the modern world, while rife with challenges, also offers unprecedented opportunities for global cooperation and understanding. Technology, which has often deepened divides, now has the potential to bridge them, creating spaces where people from diverse cultures and backgrounds can come together in shared purpose. The task before us is not simply to imagine this future but to build it—piece by piece, person by person, decision by decision.

A new era of collective humanity requires a shift in perspective—a movement away from the isolation that tribalism encourages toward the solidarity that unity fosters. This shift begins with the understanding that our individual stories are not isolated narratives but part of a larger, interconnected tapestry. The struggles of one are the struggles of all, the triumphs of one are the triumphs of all, and the future of one is the future of all. It is through this shared understanding that we begin to see the value in every life, in every experience, in every voice. In this new era, no one is left behind, no one is disregarded, and no one is viewed as less than another.

At the heart of this new era is the recognition that we are all custodians of the world we share. The ecological, social, and economic challenges we face demand a collective response. Climate change, inequality, and conflict cannot be addressed by one group, one nation, or one ideology alone. They require a unified approach, one that embraces the diversity of thought, culture, and experience but is grounded in a commitment to the collective good. In this era, true leadership is not defined by power or control, but by the ability to bring people together for a common cause, to inspire cooperation, and to elevate the values of empathy, justice, and sustainability.

The shift toward a new era of collective humanity also calls for a reimagining of what it means to belong. Belonging is no longer confined to one's family, tribe, or nation, but extends to the global community. In this vision, the world is not a collection of competing groups but a single, vast network of interconnected lives, each one contributing to the whole. This vision does not require the abandonment of cultural identities or personal histories but invites individuals to expand their sense of belonging beyond the immediate and the familiar to encompass all of humanity.

This new era of collective humanity is marked by shared values, but also by the recognition of the beauty and strength of diversity. Rather than seeking to erase differences, this era seeks to celebrate them, recognizing that the richness of human experience—our languages, traditions, customs, and beliefs—is what makes the world vibrant and dynamic. In this vision, diversity is not a barrier to unity but a reflection of it. It is through understanding and embracing our differences that we find the strength to move forward together.

The future of collective humanity is also shaped by the spirit of innovation and collaboration. As we face increasingly complex global challenges, we will need to harness the creativity, intelligence, and ingenuity of every individual. This is an era where solutions are found not through isolation but through collective effort. It is an era where every person has the opportunity to contribute their gifts, where collaboration becomes the norm, and where the collective wisdom of humanity is used to solve the greatest problems we face.

The journey into this new era is not without obstacles, and the road ahead is not always clear. Yet, the path is paved with hope—the hope that through our shared struggles, our collective efforts, and our commitment to each other, we can create a world where unity is not just a dream, but a reality. It is a world where every individual is valued, every voice is heard, and every life is seen as part of the greater whole. The new era of collective humanity is a vision waiting to be realized, and it begins with each of us—choosing to live with empathy, to act with justice, and to love with purpose. The work is long, but the rewards are beyond measure, for in this journey, we will not only change the world, but we will transform ourselves along the way.

The Power of Collective Action

The journey toward a unified, collective humanity rests on the profound power of collective action. There is a force that arises when individuals come together with a shared purpose, a synergy that propels humanity toward progress in ways that would be impossible through isolated efforts. This power, however, is not automatic; it requires intentionality, cooperation, and a vision that transcends personal gain for the greater good. When the collective will aligns with a shared vision, transformation is not just possible—it becomes inevitable.

Collective action is rooted in the simple yet powerful idea that we are stronger together. In small communities, this can look like neighbors coming together to support one another, whether through a shared meal, a helping hand, or an open ear. In larger contexts, collective action becomes more complex, addressing issues that span beyond the individual and the local: global challenges such as climate change, poverty, social injustice, and the preservation of peace. These issues require a coming together of minds, resources, and efforts from all corners of the world, transcending borders, tribes, and ideologies.

One of the most striking examples of the power of collective action lies in social movements throughout history. From the civil rights movement in the United States to the global campaigns for women's suffrage, collective action has shifted the course of history. These movements began with a single voice—one person standing up for justice—but it was through the collective voice of millions, each contributing their energy, their resources, and their passion, that real, lasting change was achieved. The success of these movements was not based on the strength of one individual but the strength of many, united by a shared vision of equality and justice.

Similarly, the global effort to combat pandemics, like the response to COVID-19, demonstrates how collective action, powered by science, empathy, and solidarity, can overcome even the most daunting challenges. While the virus spread across borders, so too did the collective response—from healthcare workers risking their lives on the frontlines to scientists working together across continents to develop vaccines. Communities pulled together in unprecedented ways, proving that when humanity is united in purpose, even the darkest times can be met with hope and action.

Yet, collective action is not just about responding to crises. It is also about the everyday choices we make to work together, to support one another, and to invest in building communities that are inclusive, compassionate, and resilient. It is in the choices to listen, to understand, and to take action on behalf of those who need it most. Whether it is providing for the homeless, advocating for the voiceless, or simply sharing time and resources with others, collective action takes shape in a myriad of small and large ways, all contributing to the betterment of society.

However, the power of collective action cannot be fully realized without a shared commitment to the values that will guide it. Justice, compassion, integrity, and a deep respect for the dignity of every person are the foundational principles that must underlie any collective effort. Without these values, collective action risks becoming misguided or distorted, driven by personal gain or ideological loyalty rather than the pursuit of the common good.

For collective action to be truly effective, it requires that each individual sees themselves as part of the larger whole—not as separate from it. The sense of individual responsibility to the group is essential, but so is the recognition that the well-being of others is tied to one's own. When we act in the interest of others, we not only elevate the collective but also enrich our own lives. The bonds that form through shared action create a sense of belonging, of purpose, and of meaning that transcends the isolation and division that often plague modern society.

The potential of collective action is immense. If humanity can unite across its differences, if we can channel the power of cooperation, empathy, and shared purpose, we have the ability to create a world marked by peace, justice, and sustainability. The road to this future is not easy, but it is possible. And it begins with each of us—the decisions we make, the actions we take, and the way we choose to see the world and our place in it. Through collective action, we can shape a future where unity is not just a vision, but a living, breathing reality.

The Enduring Promise of Unity

The enduring promise of unity is not found in perfect harmony or the absence of conflict, but in the unwavering belief that together, we can overcome the forces that seek to divide us. It is a promise that speaks to the deep and timeless yearning within the human spirit—a yearning to connect, to belong, and to create something greater than the sum of our parts. This promise, when embraced, has the potential to transform not only the world we live in but also the very nature of who we are as individuals and communities.

Unity is not a passive condition. It is a dynamic force, one that requires effort, intentionality, and a shared commitment to building bridges, not walls. It demands that we step outside the confines of our comfort zones, challenge our assumptions, and move beyond the limits of tribal loyalty to embrace a more expansive and inclusive vision of what it means to belong. True unity is forged in the spaces between our differences, where empathy, respect, and understanding converge to create something that transcends division.

This promise of unity is not idealistic or naïve; it is rooted in the knowledge that while division is natural, it is not inevitable. Throughout history, humanity has risen above its divisions to achieve extraordinary feats—whether it was the collaboration required to land a man on the moon, the global response to humanitarian crises, or the victories won through social movements that changed the course of justice. These moments of unity remind us that when we come together, we are capable of achieving what may have once seemed impossible.

Yet, the road to this enduring unity is neither easy nor straightforward. There are forces—both internal and external—that seek to pull us back into the comfort of division. Tribalism, with its promise of security and belonging, continues to offer an alluring path, one that often comes at the cost of the broader connection we are all capable of. But the promise of unity calls us to resist this pull, to challenge the narratives that seek to define us solely by the tribe we belong to, and to instead embrace the greater narrative of shared humanity.

This enduring promise is also a call to action. It challenges us to see beyond ourselves, to prioritize the well-being of others, and to work toward a world where everyone has a place. It requires us to look at the divisions that exist in our world—not as insurmountable walls but as opportunities for connection, for learning, and for growth. The promise of unity is realized every time we choose compassion over judgment, collaboration over competition, and understanding over fear. It is in these moments, however small, that we build the foundation for a more unified world.

In this unified world, our differences are not erased but celebrated. The diversity of thought, culture, and experience is not a threat to our unity, but its greatest strength. When we choose unity, we choose to see the richness that each individual and community brings to the global tapestry. We recognize that the uniqueness of every person enhances the collective whole, and that true unity is not the blending of sameness but the harmony of difference. It is a world where the diversity of the human experience is cherished, where collaboration fosters innovation, and where understanding and compassion are the bedrock of society.

The promise of unity is not simply about bringing people together—it is about elevating humanity to a higher vision, one that values both the individual and the collective. It is a vision that allows each person to contribute their gifts, their passions, and their perspectives, knowing that their contribution is vital to the success and flourishing of all. In this vision, we are not isolated tribes, but one human family, bound together by shared values, goals, and a commitment to one another's well-being.

The enduring promise of unity is a vision we can all work toward, a vision that calls us to live with purpose, with empathy, and with a recognition that our interconnectedness is the greatest source of strength we possess. It is a promise that, when fully realized, will transform not just the world around us but the very nature of our relationships, our communities, and our global society. The promise of unity is not a distant dream, but a living, breathing reality that begins within each of us, in every act of kindness, every moment of understanding, and every choice to build bridges instead of walls.

The Eternal Quest for Belonging

At the heart of the human experience lies an eternal quest—the search for belonging. From the moment we are born, we are drawn to the presence of others, to the warmth of connection, the safety of community, and the affirmation of being known. This deep-seated need is woven into the very fabric of our souls, and it is one of the most powerful forces shaping our identities, our choices, and our relationships. Yet, this quest for belonging is also fraught with tension, as the instinct to belong can lead to division, exclusion, and the creation of boundaries that separate rather than unite.

The quest for belonging begins in the first moments of life. A child, helpless and vulnerable, reaches out for the comforting embrace of a caregiver, seeking connection as a fundamental need for survival. As the child grows, this need extends beyond the family to the broader world. The desire to belong is no longer satisfied solely by proximity to loved ones but by the formation of larger communities—tribes, cultures, and nations—that offer a sense of purpose, identity, and security. It is through these connections that we come to understand who we are and where we fit within the vast tapestry of humanity.

Yet, belonging within a group is not without its challenges. The very nature of tribalism—our instinctive tendency to form in-groups and out-groups—creates boundaries that can be both protective and restrictive. These boundaries, while offering a sense of security and solidarity, also define who is "in" and who is "out," creating divisions that often lead to judgment, exclusion, and even hostility. The desire to belong, if left unchecked, can transform into an obsession with tribal loyalty, an unwillingness to see others outside our group as equally worthy of connection, empathy, and love.

This dynamic plays out in both personal and societal spheres. As individuals, we may find ourselves drawn to groups that align with our values, our interests, or our identities, seeking out those who share our vision of the world. In doing so, we often reinforce the boundaries that separate us from those who do not share our beliefs or experiences. The desire to belong, though natural, can quickly slip into a form of exclusivity that fosters division. In our pursuit of unity within our tribe, we can inadvertently contribute to the very division we seek to overcome.

The question, then, becomes how we can honor our need for belonging without falling into the trap of division. How can we cultivate connection that transcends the boundaries of our tribes and embraces the shared humanity of all people? The answer lies not in rejecting the tribe but in expanding it—recognizing that the quest for belonging can be a force for good when it is rooted in inclusivity, empathy, and understanding.

The eternal quest for belonging is not only about finding our place within a tribe but about understanding that true belonging encompasses the entire human family. Belonging is not confined to those who think like us, act like us, or live like us. It extends to every individual, regardless of race, creed, or background. To belong is to recognize that we are part of something larger than ourselves, something that includes every voice, every story, and every experience.

In this light, the quest for belonging becomes a call to transcend the limitations of tribalism and embrace a vision of unity that honors diversity. It asks us to see the connections between us, even in the face of differences, and to build a world where belonging is not about exclusivity but inclusivity—a world where every person is welcomed, valued, and seen. True belonging is not about who is inside the circle but about how wide that circle can grow, how many lives it can touch, and how deeply it can connect us all.

The quest for belonging, when rooted in the recognition of our shared humanity, has the power to heal wounds, mend divisions, and create a world where unity is not a distant ideal but a living reality. It is a quest that will continue as long as humanity exists, an ongoing journey to find not only where we belong but to create spaces where everyone belongs. As we move forward on this path, may we remember that the true essence of belonging lies not in the boundaries we create, but in the connections we forge—connections that transcend the divisions of tribe, culture, and ideology and embrace the shared dignity of every human being.

The Power of Hope and Action

Hope is the spark that ignites change; it is the quiet but unwavering belief that a better world is possible. Yet hope, in its truest sense, is not passive—it is a call to action. It is a force that compels us to not only imagine a world of unity and connection but to actively participate in creating it. The journey toward a united future, a world where empathy and collaboration are the driving forces, begins with each person making the conscious choice to move beyond division and toward the shared dream of collective humanity.

Hope, when fueled by action, has the power to reshape reality. It propels us to take those first steps into uncomfortable spaces, to challenge the biases and prejudices that have long governed our thoughts and actions. It empowers us to see the humanity in others, even in those who appear vastly different from ourselves. It encourages us to transcend the tribal instinct that separates and instead embrace the universal truth that we are all part of the same human family. Hope asks us to believe in the possibility of connection, even when the barriers to that connection seem insurmountable.

But hope must be accompanied by action if it is to manifest in the world. It is easy to be swept away by the current of fear, mistrust, and division that often surrounds us. Yet, hope remains an active choice, one that requires us to step into the spaces where unity is most needed. Action begins in the smallest moments—choosing understanding over judgment, compassion over indifference, dialogue over silence. Every action, no matter how small, contributes to the larger movement toward unity.

In communities, hope and action combine to create transformative change. Grassroots efforts to bridge divides, to bring together people from different backgrounds, and to address the needs of the marginalized are the building blocks of a unified society. These efforts, while often quiet and unseen, have the power to alter the fabric of society, creating new spaces where people can come together and work toward the common good. Whether it's through educational initiatives, social justice movements, or local activism, these acts of collective action are the heartbeat of a movement for unity.

On a larger scale, hope and action inspire political and societal change. Leaders, both elected and community-driven, have the power to mobilize people toward collective goals, using their influence to advocate for justice, equality, and peace. The hope for a better world must be channeled into policies that reflect the values of inclusivity and compassion, ensuring that every individual, regardless of their background, has the opportunity to thrive. It is through this combination of leadership and collective action that societal divisions can be addressed and lasting unity can be established.

Hope also fuels the work of reconciliation. As we look to the past, we cannot ignore the injustices and divisions that have shaped our world. However, the power of hope lies in its ability to guide us toward healing. Reconciliation requires that we confront the painful truths of history, acknowledge the wrongs that have been committed, and take responsibility for the actions that have perpetuated division. But reconciliation also requires forgiveness—the willingness to let go of the past in order to build a future based on trust and mutual respect. Hope leads us through this difficult process, reminding us that unity is not about forgetting the past but learning from it and using that knowledge to create a better future.

The path forward, then, is illuminated by both hope and action. Hope reminds us that unity is possible, that we can create a world where all people are valued and respected. Action ensures that this hope is not just an abstract concept, but a living reality that grows stronger with every choice we make. By choosing hope, by choosing to act in service of others, we contribute to the larger movement toward collective humanity, one that is bound not by division, but by the shared dream of a united, compassionate, and just world.

Hope, when coupled with action, is transformative. It gives us the strength to keep moving forward even when the journey feels overwhelming. It propels us to rise above the forces of division and to build a world where unity is not only possible but inevitable. The power of hope and action is the force that will shape the future—a future where all people, regardless of tribe, culture, or belief, can come together as one. It is a future where we are defined not by our differences, but by our shared humanity. And it begins with each of us choosing to take that first step toward unity—one act of hope, one step of action, at a time.

A Vision of Lasting Change

As we look ahead, we must carry with us the understanding that the vision of unity, though profound, is not a singular event or a final destination. It is a journey that requires constant effort, a perpetual unfolding of human potential that can only be realized if we commit ourselves to the work of lasting change. The vision of a unified world is not an unattainable dream, but a future within our reach—one that calls for our active participation, unwavering belief, and collective commitment to transforming the world into a place where love, justice, and compassion bind us all together.

True, lasting change is not the product of one grand gesture but the result of countless small, intentional actions. Every moment of kindness, every effort to bridge a divide, every decision to put the needs of the collective before the desires of the individual adds to the foundation upon which a unified world can be built. It is the accumulation of these actions that will ultimately reshape society, creating a global community where differences are celebrated and unity is the guiding principle.

This vision of change also demands that we see beyond the immediate and the personal. It asks us to look at the world not through the narrow lens of our own experiences but through the expansive lens of shared humanity. The issues we face—whether they are social, economic, or environmental—are interconnected. No single group, no isolated nation, can solve these challenges alone. Only through collective effort, guided by a shared vision of justice and equity, can we begin to address the systemic inequalities, injustices, and divisions that persist.

The power of collective action lies in its ability to unite individuals, communities, and nations toward a common cause. Yet this action must be informed by compassion, wisdom, and integrity. True change is not about power or domination; it is about lifting others up, working toward solutions that benefit everyone, and recognizing that the health and well-being of one is intrinsically linked to the health and well-being of all. When we act with this understanding, we begin to transform not only the structures around us but also the hearts and minds of those who inhabit them.

A vision of lasting change also requires the courage to confront our own limitations. It asks us to examine the biases, prejudices, and blind spots that have shaped our perceptions of others and the world. It is easy to maintain the comfort of the familiar, to hold on to the identities that our tribes offer us, but true change demands that we question these boundaries and step into new ways of thinking, relating, and acting. This process of self-reflection and transformation is essential if we are to build a world that reflects the values of empathy, respect, and unity.

The road to lasting change is not without its challenges. There will be setbacks, resistance, and moments when it feels as though the forces of division are too strong to overcome. But in these moments, it is essential to remember the power of persistence. Change is a gradual process, one that requires patience, perseverance, and the unwavering belief that unity is possible. Every effort, no matter how small, adds to the momentum of transformation. And when those efforts are joined together, the collective power of humanity can overcome even the greatest obstacles.

The vision of lasting change is not a call to perfection but a call to progress. It is about striving toward a better world, even when it feels out of reach. It is about taking responsibility for our role in shaping the future and doing so with the understanding that we are part of a larger story —a story that stretches back through the ages but also looks ahead, toward a future where unity is the norm and division the exception. This is the vision we must carry with us, not only in our hearts but in our actions, as we work to create a world that reflects the best of who we are and who we can become.

In the end, the promise of lasting change lies not in waiting for others to act, but in each of us choosing to make a difference. By aligning our actions with the values of love, justice, and unity, we can create a ripple effect that spreads far beyond our immediate circles. This is the power of collective humanity—the ability to come together, despite our differences, and work toward a future that is just, equitable, and unified. It begins with us, and it continues through us, as we create the world we all long to live in.

The Future We Create Together

The future we create together is not one dictated by fate or circumstance but one that we shape through our collective choices and actions. It is a future that hinges not on grand gestures or sweeping reforms alone, but on the everyday decisions we make to engage with one another, to listen, and to act in the spirit of empathy, understanding, and cooperation. The world we dream of, a world of unity, justice, and peace, will not emerge overnight. It will emerge through the constant, deliberate effort of individuals and communities coming together to create something greater than what exists now.

This future is grounded in the recognition that humanity, in all its diversity, is stronger when united. Each person, each community, brings something unique and invaluable to the table. The vast array of experiences, cultures, and perspectives that make up the human family are not liabilities but assets, offering the potential for rich collaboration, creative solutions, and deep empathy. Our differences, once seen as obstacles, can become opportunities for growth and understanding. In this future, we celebrate diversity not as a threat, but as a strength that enriches our shared existence.

The future we create together also rests on the values we choose to prioritize—values like love, justice, fairness, and respect. These values must guide our interactions with one another, our policies, and our systems of governance. When we choose to live by these principles, we ensure that no one is left behind, that every voice is heard, and that every individual is treated with dignity and worth. The work of unity cannot be done if these values are left by the wayside. They must be at the core of everything we do.

However, the future we create together is not one where unity is achieved by erasing differences. It is a future where our differences are acknowledged, respected, and woven into the fabric of a collective humanity. True unity does not demand uniformity—it celebrates the beauty of each person's unique contribution to the whole. Just as a symphony thrives on the diversity of instruments, so too does a unified world thrive when people from all walks of life contribute their voices to the chorus of human experience.

The path to this future requires action from all corners of society. It begins with the individual, who must choose to step beyond their comfort zone and engage with others in meaningful ways. It continues in families and communities, where relationships are built on trust, compassion, and understanding. It extends to institutions, businesses, and governments, where policies and practices must reflect the values of justice and equality. And it reaches across borders, as the global community comes together to address the shared challenges that affect us all—climate change, poverty, human rights, and peace.

As we move toward this future, we must also confront the obstacles that lie in our path. There will be resistance, both internal and external, as we work to overcome the forces of division that have long shaped our world. Fear of the other, the tendency to protect what is familiar, and the desire for power will not easily fade. But it is in these moments of resistance that our commitment to unity will be tested. It is in these moments that we must choose to persist, to continue working toward a world where the bonds of our shared humanity outweigh the divisions that separate us.

The future we create together will not be perfect. It will be a world marked by both progress and setbacks, but it will be one that reflects our highest aspirations—a world where unity is not just a dream, but a lived reality. A world where we see ourselves not as isolated tribes, but as a single human family, bound together by the shared values that define us. A world where our differences enrich rather than divide us, where justice, love, and peace are the guiding principles of all our interactions.

As we embark on this journey, we must remember that this future is not something that happens to us—it is something we make, together. Every choice, every action, every moment of connection contributes to the larger tapestry of change. The future we create together begins with the commitment to see one another, to listen, to act with kindness and compassion, and to build a world where unity is the foundation upon which all else rests. It begins now, with each of us, and it continues with every step we take toward a future where we are united not by our differences, but by the shared hope of a better world.

The Legacy We Leave Behind

As we reflect on the future we aim to create, it is essential to remember that the legacy we leave behind is not solely defined by the material achievements or the grand milestones we reach, but by the relationships we build, the values we uphold, and the choices we make in pursuit of unity and compassion. Every action we take today—whether small or significant—becomes part of the legacy we leave for future generations. It is in the way we treat one another, in the way we choose to build bridges rather than walls, that the true impact of our lives will be measured.

The legacy we leave behind is not one of isolated accomplishments but of a collective vision that transcends individual success. It is a legacy grounded in shared values—values of empathy, justice, understanding, and love. When we prioritize these values, we shape a world that is more connected, more equitable, and more compassionate. It is this vision that future generations will inherit, and it will be their task to carry it forward, building upon the foundation we lay today.

For future generations, the greatest inheritance will not be material wealth or technological advancements, but the lessons learned from our pursuit of unity and the example we set in overcoming division. The choices we make now will serve as the model for how they approach their own challenges, how they navigate differences, and how they come together to solve the problems that will inevitably arise. The world we build today will be the world they inherit tomorrow, and the values we live by will be the compass that guides them.

The legacy of unity is not a legacy of perfection but one of perseverance. It is the legacy of individuals and communities who, despite the obstacles they faced, chose to build a better world. It is the legacy of those who, in moments of conflict and division, chose reconciliation over retaliation, understanding over judgment, and love over hate. These actions, though sometimes unnoticed and uncelebrated, are the true markers of a legacy that will endure for generations.

Moreover, the legacy we leave is not confined to the immediate future but is also a timeless reminder of our shared humanity. The decisions we make now ripple outward, influencing not only the lives of those around us but the course of history. The commitment to unity that we demonstrate today will serve as a beacon of hope for future generations, guiding them toward a world where division is no longer the default and where connection, empathy, and mutual respect define the global community.

In building this legacy, we are not simply shaping a better future for ourselves but contributing to the unfolding story of human progress. Every step we take toward unity, no matter how difficult or uncertain, is a step toward a world where future generations can build on our efforts, making the journey toward collective humanity easier and more attainable for those who follow. It is in this way that our legacy endures—not in monuments or accolades, but in the lives we touch, the change we inspire, and the unity we foster.

The legacy we leave behind is not just the result of our actions, but the embodiment of our deepest values. It is a legacy of hope, of healing, and of connection—a legacy that transcends the divisions of our time and moves humanity forward toward a more just, compassionate, and unified world. The future we create today will be the world future generations live in tomorrow, and it is in our hands to make that world one of lasting unity, peace, and shared purpose.

Conclusion

The journey we have walked together through the labyrinth of tribalism has brought us face to face with the deepest currents of human nature. We have examined the primal instincts that drive us to group ourselves into tribes, seeking comfort, identity, and belonging. Yet, we have also glimpsed the possibility of a world where these same instincts, instead of dividing us, can serve as a force for unity, connection, and collective action. As we stand at the threshold of this new vision, we are called not just to reflect on what has been, but to act on what could be.

Tribalism is a force as old as humanity itself, woven into the very fabric of our existence. It has shaped our identities, determined our allegiances, and guided the course of history. But tribalism is not the final word. Though it has given rise to conflict, division, and suffering, it has also shown us the profound need for connection, for belonging, and for a sense of purpose greater than the self. In this paradox, there lies both the challenge and the opportunity for us to transcend our divisions and build a future of greater unity.

This journey, however, is not one of instant transformation. The path to reconciliation and unity is long and often fraught with setbacks. It requires an unwavering commitment to change, both on a personal level and within our communities. We must choose, daily, to move beyond our tribal instincts, to see the humanity in others, and to act in ways that foster connection rather than division. The hope of a unified world is not something that will be handed to us—it is something we must create with our own hands, through every conversation, every act of kindness, and every decision to place the common good above tribal loyalty.

As we strive for unity, we must also embrace the complexity of human identity. Unity does not mean uniformity. It is not a call for everyone to think alike or to erase the beautiful diversity that defines us. True unity, the kind that lasts, is found in the harmonizing of differences—when the varied threads of human experience are woven together into a tapestry stronger and more vibrant than any individual strand. Just as a symphony does not seek to make each instrument the same but celebrates the distinct sound each brings, so too must we celebrate our differences, knowing that together we create something far more powerful than we could ever achieve alone.

The work of building a unified world is not easy. It asks us to confront our fears, to let go of the comforts of separation, and to reach out to others with open hearts. It requires the courage to face uncomfortable truths, to question the narratives that have divided us, and to listen with empathy to the voices we have long ignored. Yet, in this work, we find our greatest potential—not in what we achieve individually, but in how we come together as a collective force for good.

But this vision, this promise of unity, does not lie in the distant future. It begins now, in the choices we make today. It is built in every moment of connection, every choice to extend empathy, every effort to break down the walls that separate us. The world we create together is not a dream—it is a reality in the making, one step at a time, one person at a time. The seeds of unity are planted in the smallest of actions, and as they take root, they spread outward, creating a movement that will one day transform the world.

As we look to the future, let us remember that the legacy we leave behind is not one defined by the divisions of our time, but by the unity we worked so tirelessly to create. The legacy of compassion, understanding, and collaboration will ripple through generations, shaping a world where the bonds of humanity are stronger than the forces that seek to divide us. The future is ours to build—a future where the walls of tribalism crumble, and in their place, we find the open, welcoming arms of a shared human family.

The road ahead is not without obstacles, but it is a road worth traveling. With every step we take, we move closer to a world where the bonds of unity are not just a hopeful ideal but a living reality. We are the architects of this world. And the promise of a unified humanity is not just a vision for the future—it is a call to action, a call to live out the values of connection, empathy, and love that will bring us together in ways that transcend the tribes we once thought defined us.

The time for action is now. Let us walk forward together, not as isolated groups, but as one human family, united in our shared purpose, and bound by the belief that together, we are capable of creating a world where every person belongs, and every voice is heard. The legacy we leave behind is the future we create today. Let us make it one of lasting unity, peace, and shared humanity.